Love Always Wins

David M. Hazen

First edition, updated August 20, 2018

ISBN-13: 978-1469961392

Copyright 2011, David M. Hazen
4349 Shadow Wood Drive
Eugene, Oregon 97405
contact: innercom@peak.org

Imagineer, Eugene City of Peace
Advisor, International Cities of Peace
Peacemaker of the Year 2011, Nobel Peace Laureate Project
PeaceBuilder Award 2011, Community Mediation Services
Certified Oregon Change Agent by governor John Kitzhaber
Notable Alumnus of Achievement, University of Minnesota
Author, *"The Stripper's Guide to Canoe-building,"* Tamal Vista, 1976

Blog URL http://davidhazen.wordpress.com/

Website for this book: *http://lovealwayswins.us/*

Cover Graphic from a painting by Fred Masarie
3355 North Delta #29, Eugene, 97408
541-687-1166   brtstk@comcast.net

Dedication

To all the children of the world,
born and unborn, and
those who would be like them.

Gratitude

I stand on the shoulders of all my teachers, mentors, and role model giants, in no particular order of priority: Buckminster Fuller, William Gregory, Oscar Ichazo, Dot Maver, Marianne Williamson, Michael Beckwith, Donna Stevens, Michael Meade, Francis Moore Lappé, Deepak Chopra, Mark Umbreit, Azim Khamisa, Riane Eisler, David Adams, Alan Briskin, Tom Atlee, David Cooperrider, Paul Ray, Burt Munro, Yvonne and Rich Dutra-St.John, His Holiness the XIVth Dalai Lama, Sheldon B. Kopp, Marcus J. Borg, Bill Wilson, John Stacey, Sterling Ellsworth, Darelle Barber, Joe Klaas, Rev. Greg Flint, and my greatest teacher of all that has no name which does it justice yet can be implied with the joyful resounding cry, "I AM!"

A special and humble gratitude goes to the wind beneath my wings, my wife Valerie, who taught me how to be a husband, and to the ones who taught me how to parent, my sons Chris and Michael.

I am deeply indebted to those who critiqued my original draft and greatly assisted me in the quality of my writing: Christopher Hazen, Phyllis Hockley, Rebecca Hazen, Gary Baran, Karen Johnson and especially to Barbara Shaw, who diligently highlighted my problems with fuzzy wording, commas and run-on sentences. I have also been blessed by the web hosting and publishing advice and services of my dear friend, Dennis Rivers.

4

Foreword by Dorothy J. Maver, PhD.

"Think with your heart."

Thanks so much to David Hazen, for these words of wisdom and for sharing his story through *Love Always Wins: Hope for Healing the Epidemic of Violence*. It is a journey of honesty, authenticity, and a testament to the power, love, and creative intelligence of the human spirit. Yes, we can break the cycle of violence.

In Love Always Wins, David takes a page out of "the book of daring" as he embodies and expresses the courage to be the change he wishes to see in the world. His personal story is a version of our collective story, a microcosm of the macrocosm.

The description of one individual's journey from living in a culture of violence to creating a personal and social culture of peace, using Mark Umbreit's *Twelve Steps of Personal Peacemaking*, is more than a good read. I recommend it for anyone seeking to heal and break the cycle of violence in their own life. You will find a wealth of information and practical recommendations.

Taking personal responsibility is a necessary first step to living a life of well-being in right relationship with self, others, and the world around us. Deep gratitude to David for wisely and lovingly taking us on his journey as he poignantly demonstrates how love prevails and that success is not spelled w-i-n. Letting go – the wisdom of going with the flow – is beautifully described as he reminds himself, and the reader, "I didn't need to push the river. I could swim in it."

During our time together with The Peace Alliance, I recall a session with State Coordinators regarding shared leadership and shared responsibility. David said afterwards, "Dot, you should write a book." I am grateful that he did.

David writes, "How we give ourselves away, how we use our energy in relationship with others, determines our true wealth." Indeed. May we all have the wisdom of the heart to offer our unique contribution on behalf of the common good.

Dorothy J. Maver, Ph.D., President, National Peace Academy USA
January 4, 2012

Dorothy J. Maver, Ph.D. is an educator and peacebuilder whose keynote is inspiring cooperation on behalf of the common good. Dot is President of the National Peace Academy in the USA, a founder of the Global Alliance for Ministries and Infrastructures of Peace, serves as Executive Director of The River Phoenix Center for Peacebuilding, and helps coordinate Push4Peace. Her work in education, politics and grassroots community organizing is focused on applied peacebuilding utilizing a shared responsibility and shared leadership model.

Love Always Wins

Hope for Healing the Epidemic of Violence

TABLE OF CONTENTS

ILLUSTRATIONS

Introduction to letting go

I begin with myself. Because of my experiments with it, I know today that love, compassion, and forgiveness always win in situations of conflict. I expect that you may have some doubts about that, especially the "always" part. How can I say such a thing? I'm not writing this to convince you of anything, I am simply asking you to connect your thoughts with your feelings and conduct your own experiment. I will not present historical, scientific, moral or legal arguments to justify my conclusions, just my story and simple logic.

Through a progression of damaging events in my childhood, I had lost my True Self, my integrity, and any sense of self-worth. I was filled with rage. At the age of 26 I wanted a rocket launcher to blow up a few things. I was spiritually violent with myself frequently, ready to commit suicide in varying degrees. At the age of 41, the anger and rage had become an enormous load of shame and guilt, as I had become physically violent with my second wife, and I had failed miserably at being a father to my son from my first marriage, in the same way my father had failed with me.

I am now 68 years old and have been following a program of recovery for 26 years. I am still married, my son tells me he loves me, I have many heart-felt friends, and I intend to live to 120 because life is so wonderful. I feel that I have broken the cycle of violence in my family, with the help of my mentors and teachers.

February, 1985

Later on I will tell the story leading up to and following the turning point of my life which occurred in February of 1985. My father had died in a hospital when I was 14, and ever since that time I had associated hospitals with death.

Now my only son Chris lay in post-operative recovery following a tracheotomy. Tubes and wires were attached to his head, chest, and arms. Fear of his death and fear of the unknown gripped my heart. The surgery was required to prevent his suffocation from a mysterious swelling in the side of his throat. The swelling bore an eerie similarity to the disease that killed my father, Hodgkin's disease. The doctors had ruled that out, and yet they didn't know what was afflicting Chris. There was no insurance coverage for what just happened. This is the son whom I had literally abandoned when I divorced Barbara 8 years previously. In spite of all my best intentions to not be like my father, the thought that my lack of responsibility was a generational repetition of paternal abandonment and possibly causing permanent harm to an innocent person was intolerable.

As I walked out of Sacred Heart Hospital, suicide weighed heavily on my mind. I was wallowing in toxic shame, guilt, and self-pity. My addiction to alcohol and other drugs had consumed not only my own life, it had also wreaked havoc in the lives of the people closest to me.

There was a glimmer of hope on my horizon if I could muster up the courage to accept treatment and somehow save my second marriage, to Valerie. Perhaps that is why I handed her the car keys, to prevent myself from driving very fast into something very solid. I saved my life by letting go of it. I had no idea that would be the outcome, I just did it without thinking much about it. My desperation led me to do something intuitive and opposed to the voices in my head that were telling me I didn't deserve to live.

This simple action of letting go would be repeated so many times in the coming years that it has become a permanent part of my lifestyle. I believe that letting go of rational control in order to include my emotions and intuition in my decision-making is both the process and the goal of my life. It doesn't matter where I am on this path of letting go, at the beginning, middle, or end of it, only that I be self-consciously on the path.

Within 24 hours of leaving the hospital, I was in another kind of hospital. I admitted myself to a treatment center for alcoholism and drug addiction. It was there that the toxic shame, guilt, and self-pity began to unravel. It was there that I began recovery from this form of self-inflicted violence, chemical dependency. I can say not only have I learned a lot about myself, I have also begun to view my fellow human beings through the lens of addiction and recovery.

Breaking the silence

In treatment, I learned that as I grew up I had unconsciously adopted the family pattern of not talking, not trusting, and not feeling in ways that are authentic. It wasn't until I became honest with myself and others, breaking those rules in recovery, that I discovered that I was not uniquely isolated in a death-oriented spiral. I found that other parents did the exact same abusive things to their kids, and even said the exact same intimidating and hurtful words as my father, "Shut up, or I'll really give you something to cry about." It was not uncommon for him to use a belt. I still have vivid memories of being whipped. One day, when I was perhaps five years old, he was so angry he probably didn't realize he had grabbed the wrong end of the belt and was hitting my butt with the buckle-end. I was terrified. I was howling with unbelievable pain. I was trying to protect myself with my hands, when the buckle struck my thumbnail, breaking it off. I started to bleed. Daddy stopped the whipping and bandaged my thumb, but he could not bandage my soul.

To this day there is an excruciatingly painful hole in my heart when I think of Daddy. I grieve the abandonment of not having the kind of father I needed.

I learned to fear and avoid Daddy like he was the devil himself. I would wake up in a sweat from scary nightmares about being pursued by a figure I never saw but knew was a devil. I became hyper-vigilant to the sound of Daddy's footsteps, and I would hear his mood in the way that he walked. I would protect myself by becoming invisible as much as possible, not rocking the boat, and never telling the truth about what I really thought or felt. I denied my feelings so much that I lost the ability to identify and talk about them. In treatment I was given a vocabulary list of feelings to help me recover my awareness of them.

I struggled in recovery to understand my father and the violence that erupted not only from him and but also from myself in spite of all my determination to never do to others what he did to me. What I learned has shaped not only my view of myself as an individual, but also my view of the culture in which I live. Seventy percent of college-educated women spank their children; other studies have found that up to 90% of all parents use corporal punishment, as my father did.[1] I believe the mind-set that drives family violence also drives the violence which continues to pour from nation-states.

Ultimately, this is a book about humanity's most pressing and overwhelming problem, how to create world peace. My definition of peace is not a destination where peace has been won. Peace is an ongoing, seemingly paradoxical process of surrender to the complex, organic evolution of stability and security in the presence of conflict. It is always a courageous seeking of the unknown. It cannot

---

[1] Rochman, B., The First Real-Time Study of Parents Spanking Their Kids, TIME, June 28, 2011, http://healthland.time.com/2011/06/28/would-you-record-yourself-spanking-your-kids

be bought with money, power, or rebellion. Peace is ours to claim, now.

I now view violence as an addictive pattern of behavior and a form of insanity, a betrayal and denial of our deepest humanity and of our natural ability to love one another. When we obsessively repeat the same mistakes over and over again, attempting to achieve a different result, that behavior is by definition insane. In my addiction, I was insane: numb, frozen in fear, unable to think or act in creative, functional ways. I could not resolve problems in ways that did not involve self-abuse or other-abuse. I could not break the cycle of violence.

I became acutely aware of how my anger was out of control one day when I screamed at a tree that would not fall in the direction that I had intended for it. I was so angry that I didn't notice the still-running chainsaw as I attempted to push the tree with all my strength. The chain cut through my pants and cut my knee open. I was still so full of adrenalin and anger, now directed at myself, that I refused help from the other men that were working with me. I drove myself 30 miles to the nearest emergency room to get stitches. How sane is that? This incident was in the early years of my active use of mood-altering chemicals. I didn't stop using for another 15 years, as my explosive rage continued to become worse.

I intend to show you in this book how the insanity, the violence and the many types of addiction that are endemic in our culture are driven by the same fear of abandonment which generated my dishonesty about my feelings. When we deny our feelings as a norm for the entire culture, we become generally crazy and obsessed with repeating cycles of conflict, split off from a great source of wisdom for resolving them. We continue to create the very isolation and abandonment that we deeply and unconsciously fear.

The public and private eruptions of anger and deadly violence that are common in our culture, the bitter conflicts between polarized political views, and the moral judgments heaped upon entire classes of people are examples of what happens when logical analysis excludes the awareness of intangible feelings. As any good car salesman will tell you, people like to think they are making intelligent, rational decisions, when in fact their decisions are 95% based on unconscious emotions, so it makes sense to be aware of our feelings.

The bombs will stop falling when
we get in touch with our emotions.

I believe the evolution of humanity demands that we take a leap into a non-rational or more emotional state of being, a non-analytical state of mind in which relationships define us, we accept and understand our emotions, and we are no longer materialistic individualists. We may be on the cusp of a paradigm shift from a culture of domination to a culture of cooperation which is the basis for peace. I am excited to be alive and part of this piece of history. The evolution of a culture of peace and nonviolence is accelerating, and many people will be taken by surprise when it breaks free of sub-culture status to become mainstream.

I see that we are entering an upward spiral of knowledge and abilities that will promote, worldwide, the healthy growth and development of children; prosperity and safety for adults; as well as cooperative learning and problem-solving. Such genius will flower that sometime in the future, as we look back at the current state of humanity, it will seem as if we were like the dodo, and we will wonder why and how we were saved from extinction.

Dissolving all the hate and uncovering the love is our key to survival, and I will present a map for that emotional journey. This is an extremely complex and difficult task for an individual, and yet it is the basis of my hope for recovery from the culture of violence. The transformation of an entire culture of millions of individuals may be beyond our ability to imagine, and yet I have experienced hotel convention rooms filled with hundreds of excited, committed, recovering men and women. I know there are thousands of these rooms around the world, none of which are reported in the mainstream media because the people in them have agreed to remain anonymous. However, the principles of recovery are documented and available to anyone who wants them. As those principles become more widely known and applied to a broad range of addictive behaviors, I am confident that there will be a massive cultural transformation.

I wrote this book primarily for my children, to share the story of my recovery from dependency on mood-altering chemicals and behaviors of control, domination, and violence. If I wish to be remembered for only one thing, it would be that I broke the cycle of violence in my family. I am no longer trapped in cycles of self-inflicted, heart-breaking violence. I am a recovering violent person and I'm still learning to walk my talk. I am faking it until I make it. This book is about how I fell and stumbled my way into a new way of living. I'm learning to fall and stumble today with a bit more gracefulness so I don't hurt myself. I am learning to roll and bounce.

As part of that learning, I wrote this book for myself, to express and refine the lessons of these years so that I understand them better. An important part of that process has been the circulation of draft copies of my manuscript. By dancing with the readers of my draft, listening to how they responded to my words, I found how incomplete my expression had been. I knew what I meant, and my message wasn't getting across. In response, I have completely re-organized the manuscript. I have to admit that I will probably never be completely understood, which is a good thing because it will keep the conversation going. My

only real mistake will be to give up and shut down, to give in to self-doubt and self-condemnation. I invite you to dance with me as we search for the answer to the question, how can we create non-violence in ourselves and peace in our world?

This book is my attempt to answer that question. Because I have become violent, I understand violence from the inside. Now my personal recovery from violence is strengthened by sharing it with others. My life of desperation has been transformed into a life of hope. Today my excitement comes from seeing myself as a member of a winning team called humanity instead of as a self-styled cowboy in competition with others.

My story is not unique. I am sure it is similar to millions of other recovering alcoholics, addicts and people afflicted with obsessive behaviors. The recovery movement is a cultural and social change. I believe how I express my understanding of that change has implications for others who wish to transform not only their own lives but also the lives of the people around them. This is my challenge to you: if I can be on the path of recovery, you can be also. If we can do it, our entire culture can do it.

I hope to give you a fresh way of looking at violence that may free you from the despair it creates, and in this way to plant a seed for our entire culture to recover from its dependency on violence as a problem-solving strategy. I believe that when we see ourselves in the context of a larger systemic process, it becomes easier for us to assume responsibility for the role we are to play, and problems that may initially seem to be overwhelming become manageable.

What is our role in a systemic process when somebody dies? We often think of death as the worst kind of separation, a kind of violence. We may feel unjustly treated, or violated, by the loss. We may see it as an act of violence against us perpetrated by God, the Universe, fate, a disease, another person, or whatever enemy we imagine to be the cause. If we do not free ourselves from that crushing despair, if we allow ourselves to be overwhelmed by it, we become stuck in a descending spiral of separation from all the things that keep us healthy and sane. If the despair that is a normal and healthy response to having our life torn apart by death is prolonged, it can become an act of violence against ourselves or others. Our role in the larger process is to learn to let go.

In 2001, I struggled with letting go of our dog, a Siberian Husky named McKenzie, who was very much like another child in the house, a rebellious adolescent child. He was a wild and aloof animal, always ready to run away, a characteristic that I saw in myself as well. However, he had some traits that I lacked. He was unconditionally playful, happy, and a great companion. I had become very attached to him.

I was about 16 years into my recovery when he was dying of liver cancer. The vet came to our house and put him down with a lethal injection as he was cradled in my arms, and I openly sobbed with my wife and son. For one of the first times in my life, I allowed myself to have the full experience of grief. I was able to give to McKenzie my feelings, something I had never been able to give to my father as he was dying. The intensity of my despair allowed me to break through my fear of crying in front of other people. This became one of the key turning points in my recovery.

Crying was not the only thing that would free me from the despair of losing McKenzie. I had heard about inter-species communication with animals, and I so much wanted to ask McKenzie how he felt about dying of cancer. I wanted to re-assure him that he was loved, something I may have not done sufficiently during his life. There was a lingering uncertainty about that. I called a psychic who connected with him in the afterlife and relayed messages

back and forth between us. My skepticism about this kind of "woo-woo stuff" caused me to record and transcribe the call for later analysis.

As I reread the transcript, I became convinced that yes, indeed, McKenzie had felt my love and caring during his life. This additional piece helped me to see that I had participated in, and was still participating in, a background process, a spiritual process, that was beyond my ability to recognize. I decided to take a workshop in animal communication to see if I could develop my awareness of this process. The workshop was held at a ranch on the high desert plateau of Eastern Oregon.

I knew that my rational, logical, scientific thinking habits are so strong that they would easily overwhelm my intuitive or spiritual feelings. However, a process of which I was completely unaware propelled me into setting myself up to be in a more receptive head space for what happened next.

I had been juice fasting for three days, which was intentional, but it seemed to be accidental that I also became sleep deprived. I stayed awake long after my usual bedtime watching the stars with excitement because I almost never see them from the cloudy Willamette Valley, where I live in Oregon. Then I could not get to sleep because my sleeping bag was not keeping me warm in the near-freezing temperatures, and I was too stubborn to go look for an open bunk and disturb other people in the middle of the night. When my stomach is empty and my mind has not rested, I cannot think very well in a rational way. My experiences became infused with subtle feelings and intuitions.

The next morning, as part of the workshop, I was instructed to go on an afternoon, exploratory "walkabout" in the sagebrush and juniper. Shortly after I began, a raven began croaking nearby and seemed to be following me. That gave me some encouragement. I had adopted the raven as my totem animal and felt a special connection with the Northwest Coast Indian stories about the raven.

Eventually I came upon several deer feeding in a meadow, and I stopped to watch from a distance. They noticed me and leisurely continued feeding. After some time, they moved away, and I marveled at their gentle grace, beauty and power. As I resumed walking, a ground squirrel came out on a branch directly in front of me and chattered as if it were addressing me. Unlike my usual self who would have walked on, I stopped and I listened. The squirrel seemed to say, "You could not have seen the grace, beauty and power of the deer unless it were already inside of you. You have seen yourself." I burst into tears as I recognized the truth of what the squirrel said.

Perhaps it wasn't the squirrel, perhaps I was only hearing an enlightened level of self-talk stimulated by an unlikely orchestration of external events. The mechanics of how this realization came to me does not matter to me. I learned to accept myself as having more positive characteristics than I had previously been willing to accept. Moreover, I began to see myself as an integral part of an expanding, evolving, dynamic, supportive and collaborative system of events and experiences. I am not alone. I am not doing this life all by myself. I can perhaps relax the struggle a bit and trust the process, trust my intuitive feelings.

For me, the truly important changes that we value do not occur in linear space and time, they occur in our hearts, in a way that makes space and time trivial. When we open our hearts, we not only change our perception of the present by accepting our place in a larger universe, we also change our perception of the past through forgiveness and reconciliation. In addition, we change our path into the future through a vision of hope and the courage to step forward into it. What I learned on my walkabout is that when I open myself to these kinds of non-linear messages, they are there for me. I have had a

few spontaneous, wonderful, and mysterious moments of animal communication since this time, and only when I wasn't "trying" to make it happen.

My despair about McKenzie is gone. I see his life and death in the context of a much larger series of events, all of which were gifts to my life and my recovery. His death opened the door for me to appropriately grieve the death of my mother a few years later. My connection to that dog extends beyond the grave. Although I can recall the pain of the moment of his death, I can let it go with blessings for all that I have learned about myself and for the acceptance I have for the largely unseen, unknowable system of events which supports my growth in very unexpected ways.

One of the big surprises in my journey has been a radical turnaround in my ideas about who I am.

I am not who I thought I was

We are not on solid ground
We are not solid
We are entangled with every particle
We are neither "on" nor "off"
We are the energy of motion itself
E-motion

I share with you here two edited journal entries, written in my 25th year of recovery, to illustrate the change that has occurred in my ability to identify feelings and intuitions, to be present, and to let go of the past.

January, 2010

Heaven wafts gently in and out of my awareness, people speak to me like angels, I see gardens as alternate Universes, time no longer exists as a concern, I look in the mirror and see someone I've never seen before. Some days are not like that if I become immersed in solving a "problem" until I let the solution arrive on its own when I'm not looking.

I can hardly believe I'm writing this stuff. A year ago I would have no idea what someone was talking about if they said these things.

April, 2010

I have been obsessively involved with the peace movement since 2005, going to national conferences, lobbying the offices of my senators and representatives in Washington, processing massive amounts of information about building peace, creating publicity, organizing local and state efforts, raising money and donating thousands of my own. I was heavily invested. Now, I was wrestling with a story of a world gone wrong, terribly wrong, the story of the world I live in, a world where both systemic and personal violence are so normal that most people have become numb to the accumulated damage.

All day I was listless and bored. The longer the day dragged on, the more I became depressed. That evening I went to Dances of Universal Peace with a faint hope that I would be somehow restored. The theme of the Dances that evening was all about relationship, community, renewal, and transformation. It happened that as we danced I allowed my tears to flow freely for the sad state of the world. I saw my reflection in a window as if I were a ghost, far away. "Who am I in this situation?" seemed to be the question. I was transported into a space of no time, and strange to say, my watch stopped for almost an hour before it restarted itself.

I continued to process my question sub-consciously during the night while I slept. I had a dream about coming home to a half-burnt house surrounded by firemen who were cleaning up and leaving. They had put out the fire but the house was damaged by smoke and water. I went inside and walked on wet carpet. In the corner was a magnificent tiger, cowering in fear.

When I awoke at 4 AM, I asked myself what it meant, and the answer was immediate. Before the literal light of dawn came the dawn of understanding. I was feeling the peace movement (the house) had been damaged, the state of the world was damaged, and the leadership (the tiger) was frightened.

Then the essential question, who am I in this situation, had an answer. Clear thoughts began pouring through my head, begging to be written down so I would not forget. I recalled the time when I began my recovery. I didn't know that what I wanted, or lacked, was self-acceptance, but that's what I got. I wanted comfort for not being "good enough" and comfort for being a victim of my family of origin, my culture of origin, my species of origin. I had just wanted to be comfortable with myself, accept myself just the way I am, and not be a victim of my own thoughts.

I thought I was a very weak and stupid person, a misfit, a miscreant. I didn't belong here. I thought I was alone in this world, living in hell. I saw myself as very powerless at controlling others and preventing them from hurting me except by being the violent and evil person who knew how to hurt them in return.

In recovery from chemicals, co-dependency and violence, I learned to shut down my whirling thoughts, sit down and listen. I felt in myself a growing ability to listen. At first I listened only with my ears, I heard things that I couldn't understand. Then I listened with my mind; I thought about things. Now I listen with my heart, and I feel things.

I had to speak my truth about how much I hated myself. I had to tell someone, I had to tell a whole group of people. I had to hear myself say these things and believe that someone heard me. Then I discovered I wasn't talking to myself. I heard others telling their story that was so much like my own story, reflecting it back to me. I was stunned. I stopped thinking so much. I felt connected, and the empty void within me became a solid thing with a path and a purpose. I no longer had to understand all of the violence that had happened to me with the urgency that I had felt. I felt secure in this container called recovery. I could relax, unwind, move when I felt like moving, and look at scary memories only when I was ready.

I realized that I am not who I thought I was. I am We. I am no longer a solitary, struggling, panicking idiot. At any time I can call upon the strength of all of humanity, the courage of all of humanity, or the love of all of humanity. My history still haunts me like a ghost sometimes, but now I see it only faintly at a distance, and it does not frighten me. I am not my history, in fact there is not much of me left anywhere and it's becoming difficult for me to say who I am. I seem to be just a nucleus of a large cloud of relationships. My wealth, my health, is invested and embodied in my relationships to everybody and everything, visible and invisible. So who I am has become very "fuzzy" and transient, changing moment by moment. I am not solid. I am not empty. I am not even who I think I am. I no longer know, nor do I care. This kind of uncertainty about myself seems related to the ability to choose my actions instead of reacting from my past. I feel deeply grateful for the serenity and freedom this has given me.

"The most strongly enforced of all known taboos is the taboo against knowing who or what you really are behind the mask of your apparently separate, independent, and isolated egos." -- Alan Watts[2]

Love is letting go

My recovery seems to revolve around one central concept: living in right relationship. When I relax my defenses enough, when I shut down my whirling thoughts and just listen, I can begin to see my interdependence and connections with my social, physical, and meta-physical environment. I am much more likely to creatively work *with* my relationships instead of competitively or violently against them. I no longer have to struggle to be "good enough." I can accept myself and my place in the world. The excitement of this process is what contributes the most to my happiness. Early in my recovery I got a taste of what that could be like.

In those early years I was still processing the fear and anger about leaving my old lifestyle behind. I was hanging on to memories of the comforts I had received from drugs and alcohol. I had not been willing to celebrate on my first or second anniversaries of the day I stopped using. When I passed my third anniversary, however, I truly accepted a celebration of that event with good friends in my 12-step support group. I reflected how miraculous it seemed that I could feel confident and optimistic without drugs or alcohol, that I could talk about my feelings, that I was even alive after so many incidents in which I could have been killed, and that these changes all felt so real, so authentic.

During that third year of recovery, I struggled with many issues as I entered an internship to be a treatment counselor. Trying to help those who were beginners on the path to recovery pushed me into growing and changing. I learned active listening skills that have proven useful in all areas of my life. I became a student of listening to my emotional and gut reactions to what others were saying.

---

[2] Watts, A., The Book on the Taboo Against Knowing Who You Are, Vintage Books, 1989

My image of a Higher Power had begun to shift from an angry, punishing giant like my father to a more gentle and understanding being without form. I had a memorable spiritual experience just before Christmas one year, when I was feeling particularly depressed about being an introvert and a loner. Valerie, my wife, seemed so extroverted with so many friends with whom she would go to lunch. I was comparing my insides to her outsides, and feeling stuck in the patterns of my past. So I decided that when I went for a walk with our dog, McKenzie, that I would imagine my Higher Power to be walking along with us, and I would talk to him. As I dove into talking about my feelings, tears welled up, and this went on for a few minutes of narcissistic dwelling on my failure to be an extrovert. Suddenly, I felt this message, almost like a voice speaking clearly to me, "You are OK just the way you are," and I literally stopped in my tracks. I couldn't help but in that moment accept that I was accepted by my Higher Power. I wept with relief.

I didn't stop being an introvert, and I don't suppose I ever will. However, I relaxed about it, stopped beating myself up about it, and within a few days I found myself being able to talk more easily with people I didn't know, make small talk, and enjoy it. I discovered I had an extrovert side to myself, after all. To me this was nothing short of a miracle and Valerie continues to tell me to this day how social I have become.

Today I feel the excitement and happiness about being alive that comes directly from my experiences of internal change, like this one. Generally, they have been experiences of letting go of my past self-image and accepting myself just as I am. This has always made it easier for me to accept others just as they are, and to love them for who they are today.

---

3 Rubin, T., The Angry Book, Touchstone, 1998.

Letting Old Vanity Evaporate

According to one of my friends, I have an unconventional definition of love. It is not limited to the ephemeral, situational mood, sentiment or body sensation of compassion, although that may occur within the process. Love is bigger than that. This love that I speak of is an active, engaged, sweeping, powerful process extended over time. For me, love begins with learning to be my own best friend and counselor so that I may eventually become a genuine lover of other people. Love is being in authentic, honest, detached relationship with myself and others. It is doing the work of self-care and turning it outwards into the practices of forgiveness, empathy, and compassion, simply letting go of the stuff that forms my ego and vanity of self-centered isolation, opinions and judgments. It is replacing narcissism with healthy relationships that meet everyone's needs.

My first major experience of letting go occurred just before the hospitalization of my son described in the first pages of this book. Only a few days prior to that incident, I admitted that I had a problem with drugs and alcohol. I was absolutely certain that I was not an addict or alcoholic, in spite of all the evidence to the contrary. However, I was extremely depressed, to the point of being suicidal. I was hitting my psychological bottom.

On January 23, 1985, my pot supply ran out, and it never occurred to me that I might never again resume smoking. I simply resolved to try one more time to quit, to see if I could do it. I soon felt so much anger that I curled up in bed, crying, and refused to get up. I finally began to read *The Angry Book*[3] and saw myself as a deeply angry and repressed person. I thought if I just took care of my anger, the pot smoking would go away naturally. Maybe it was time to ask for help. I made a series of phone calls to psychotherapists, and none of them wanted to deal with drug withdrawal problems. I began to drink some wine. Beer tasted bad. I coughed black chunks of phlegm from my lungs, which was frightening. As I learned later, there are far more carcinogenic substances in marijuana than in tobacco, and the bong smoking in which I had engaged did not filter out *anything*.

On February 7, I went to an intake interview for an outpatient treatment program. Together, we reviewed my history of consuming alcohol and drugs, and they told me I might have to give up my pot-smoking friends and my marriage. This was so threatening that I dove into a bottle of gin and what would be my last drunk.

However, the interviewer had suggested that I try going to a 12-step recovery group meeting that was being held in a room at an inpatient treatment center, and I went. I was moved by the honesty and eloquence of people who were struggling with apathy, alienation, and anger. I saw they were just like me. They were going around the room, speaking by turns, and everyone would introduce themselves by their name and the words "and I am an addict." I was freaking out. What if I said I was not an addict? I compromised in a way that was honest. I introduced myself for the first time in my life as an addict and added that I was having a hard time with that word. Reluctantly, I had let go of the certainty that I was not an addict.

I was also impressed with the professional, safe atmosphere of the treatment center. I asked for an intake interview, hoping they would recommend outpatient treatment. However, when Lois had finished ticking off all the twenty yes-no questions that would qualify me as a full-blown, serious addict-alcoholic, I was in tears and quickly agreed to a 30-day

inpatient program. I was ready to be cared for, I was willing to let help in.

For most of my life, the self-centered, narcissistic illusions that I carry about myself have been responsible for blocking the flow of love, either going out or coming in. The recovery process described in this book didn't teach me to love directly, it guided me to places of safety where I could let go, where I could get out of my own way. I compare it to a process so soft and gentle it is like the un-balling of a fist, or evaporation of water from a dish. That metaphor has become an acronym for me, where the letters of L.O.V.E. represent Letting Old Vanity Evaporate. I use vanity here to mean self-absorption, self-obsession, and arrogance. Evaporation is about slowly learning to surrender to the present moment, trusting oneself and others. The act of surrender opens the doorway to affection, empathy, compassion, and gratitude.

Empathy is the ability to stand in another's place, creating a safe container that could draw a supposed enemy forward and expose themselves physically, emotionally, or intellectually. This provides an opening to help them understand a better strategy to meet their needs. In order to do this, I have to be self-assured of my own security, allowing myself to be open, honest, vulnerable, without defenses, and have a curiosity about them. I have to step back from my fears and see us as united in one process of growing and learning together. I gain tremendous courage from the knowledge that I am completely safe, I have no real enemies, my integrity cannot be destroyed by them.

It takes self-empathy and self-respect for my essential humanity to create the courage to detach from my vanity. When vanity's gone, what surfaces is incredible gratitude and love for all my relationships. When I am immersed in the process of love, I feel very excited, happy, and grateful to be alive. I can see the presence of love everywhere. If I see it in me, I see it in you, and there is no separation. I am We. This becomes a victory of sorts, this feeling of being free of the oppression of my opinions and judgments, of being fully alive and in proper relationship to my social, physical, and metaphysical environment. So A.L.I.V.E. has become for me another acronym, for Aware of Love Incarnate Victorious Everywhere. The victory is in me, and I see it reflected back to me. This is what I mean by "win." When I win, when I let go of my own inner limitations, all my relationships win, everybody wins, including my so-called enemies.

The title of this book, "Love Always Wins," is not about how to compete for getting what I want out of my relationships, how to extract the goodies. Nor is it limited to a description of how relationships work at their best when the goodies are shared. It is to me a description of how I evolve, change, and grow. As far as I know, there is no other way, there is no shortcut, to learning how to love than surrendering to the process, letting go of old self-serving fears, defenses, and rigid beliefs; letting go of narcissism. The process of learning to love, Letting Old Vanity Evaporate, is a constant demand of the Universe. Lessons are repeated until learned, and I believe eventually everyone *will* learn. Thus, "Love Always Wins" is the law, L.A.W. My natural yearning as a human being is to be a lover, to be beloved, and to be love itself.

I have a choice about participating in this process or resisting it. I have a choice about letting go, trusting the unknown, overcoming my fears.

I have discovered that if I dare to do what is difficult, what I doubt will work, what frightens me, what I am not fully prepared to do, because I believe it is right, because I feel passionately that it is important, then the wind will be at my back, doors will open, connections will be made, and progress will become visible.

"When an old culture is dying, the new culture is created by those people who are not afraid to be insecure." – Rudolph Bahro

In other words, when we surrender to chaos and uncertainty, without attempting to control it, we exert a powerful, positive influence on the emergence of creative resolutions.

It has been said many times in many places: love trumps violence and unnecessary fears block our ability to love. This book describes a pathway to restoring the trust in love. Regaining trust may be the most significant and meaningful "non-achievement" of our lives. I say it in quotes because in our language "achievement" brings up images of struggle, effort, trials and errors. Learning to love for me has sometimes been best when lessons were contained in fun, laughter, dancing, jokes and tricks.

Obviously, it is not easy to be so lighthearted about something that has had serious consequences when it was missing. I think you will agree with me that for many of us we are slow learners when it comes to love and relationships. However, this is not a how-to manual of instruction. Even though I hope you may relate to my stories of mistakes and learning, I will let you make up your own self-instructions. Between us, there is a collective wisdom. Learning to love by getting out of our self-centeredness is not something that we can do on our own.

"For the trouble is that we are self-centered, and no effort of the self can remove the self from the centre of its own endeavor."
-- William Temple

Evolutionary Model of Transformation

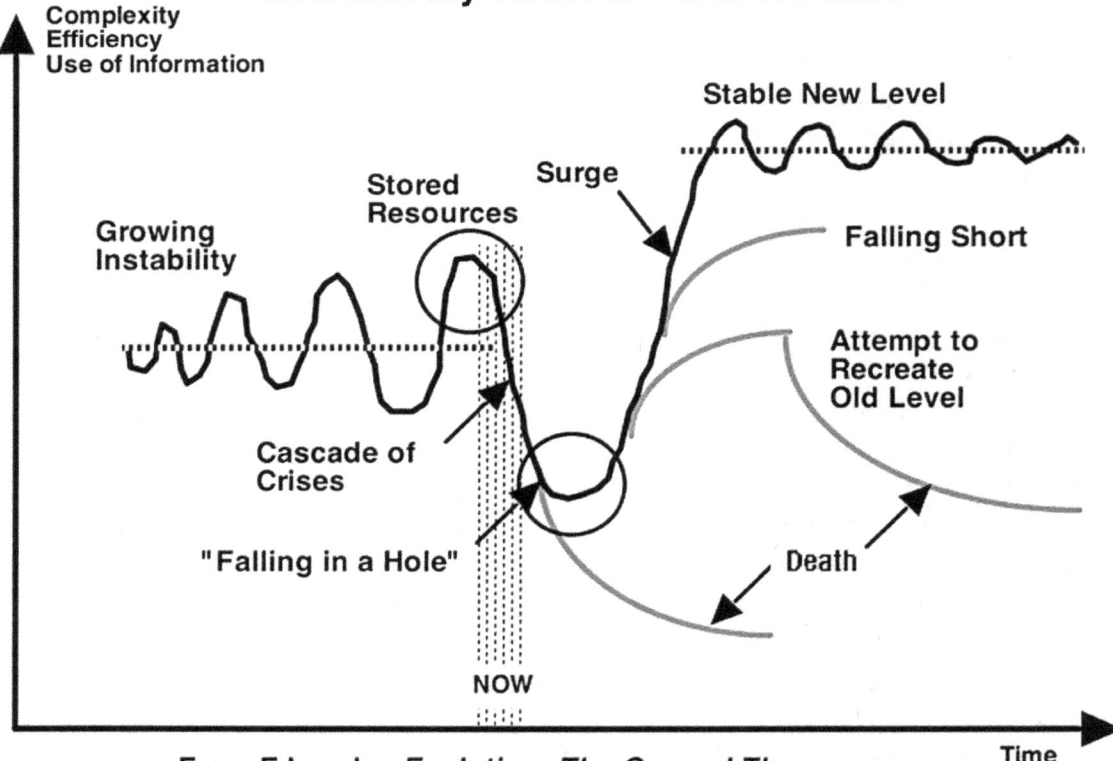

From E.Laszlo, *Evolution: The General Theory*

David Hazen's Personal Journey of Addiction & Recovery

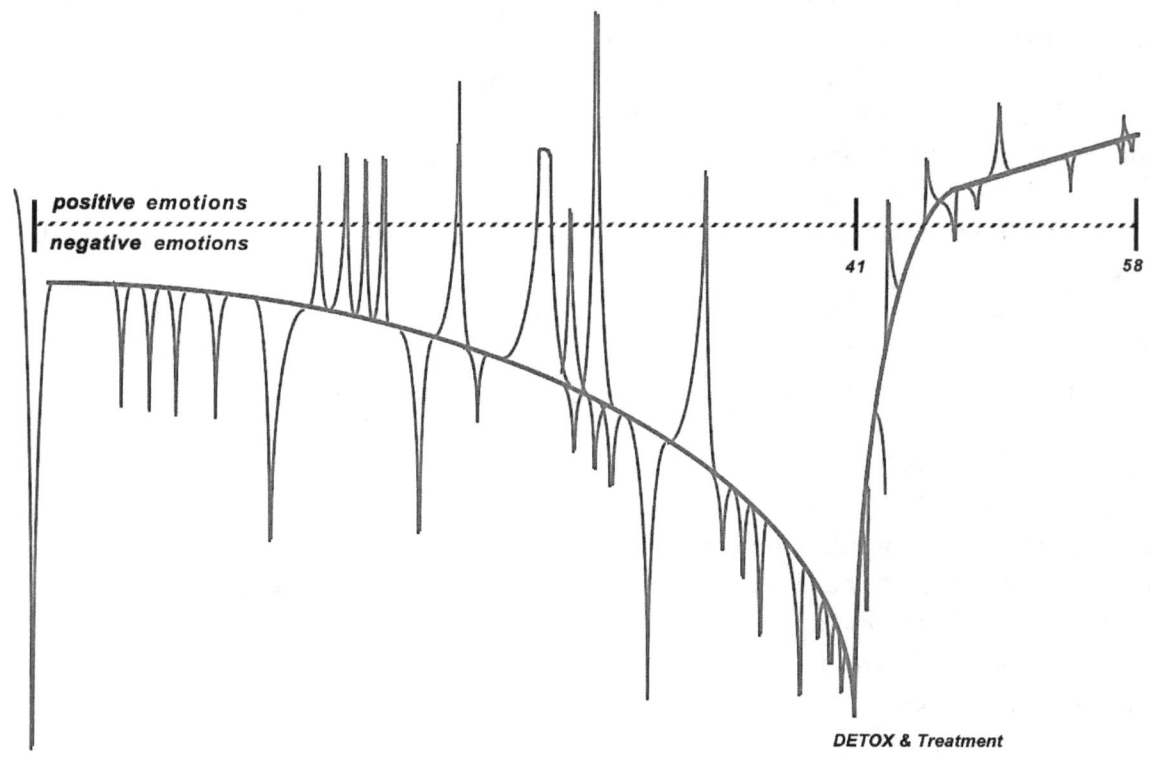

Seeking stability

To summarize what I've said about letting go, there is an intense, exciting and positive involvement in the process of learning, growing and evolving when you and I respond to a crisis of fear and uncertainty with relaxed, alert empathy for ourselves and others. I will talk about the particular crisis of violence, and first I want to establish a conceptual framework for the learning process that leads to stability.

A comparison of the two graphs on the facing page suggests that the macrocosmic process of cultural learning mirrors the microcosmic process of the individual. Systems theorist Ervin Laszlo says that living systems are self-correcting toward stability when they get out of equilibrium. His graph "Evolutionary Model of Transformation" demonstrates that a person, group, or species will literally "hunt" in chaotic and unpredictable fluctuations as it seeks a more efficient, complex, and more successful way of life.

Organic systems tend to overcorrect in both positive and negative ways until the entire system meets a threat to its survival that it cannot resolve with the tools and information it has available. In 1987, Laszlo asserted that the human species behaves as one united system and is entering an extremely destabilizing era in its history, the outcome of which is not certain.[4]

I believe that the creation of nuclear weapons in 1945 has been a major trigger for this latest plunge into dark anxiety. Today, climate change is an additional trigger of this kind of crisis because its true nature is a mass extinction event that was inadvertently set into motion by a culture of conquest. Humanity may simply die from its inability to resolve these issues, or make a new effort at stability that is incomplete. However, if enough information gets integrated rapidly, *Homo sapiens* could leap to a new level of functioning. History and fossil records show us many examples of a sudden shift in the form or function of a species or a culture when a particularly big crisis ends a long period of stability.

Now compare Laszlo's graph with the illustration of my addiction and recovery. After I had been in recovery for about ten years, I was asked by my treatment center to speak to the new patients about my personal story. I agreed to do so on a regular basis, about 4 times a year. As I retold my story, I continued to look for better ways to provide those patients with the hope that they, too, could recover. I drew the graph on the opposite page as an illustration of the progression of my disease of chemical dependency and violence. It shows how I lost and regained control of my emotional stability. Above the horizontal line are positive emotions, below it are negative emotions. The V-shaped line that reverses direction at detox and treatment is the baseline for the emotional story of my life. At the time I drew this graph I was unaware of Laszlo's drawing, and yet they are remarkably similar.

What I want you to notice about this graph is the sharp spikes up and down away from the baseline, representing the emotions tied to specific incidents. These spikes had an overall tendency to become more extreme with the passage of time. Towards the end of my active using, there are no positive emotional events, only a plunge into what is known as "hitting bottom," an extreme emotional low point, just before I accepted inpatient treatment. Notice also that in the recovery phase, there is a rapid change to a new level of functioning in a very short period of time as I learned new lifestyle habits. The emotional swings are much less extreme. The stability of my emotions today is a personal experience of peace.

4 Laszlo, E., Evolution: The Grand Synthesis, Shambhala, Boston, 1987.

On the other hand, my life began in the panic of abandonment. My family relationships gradually accumulated massive damage long before I indulged in alcohol and drugs. It was not until I was 18 years old that I began my 23-year use of mood-altering chemicals. The using was a vain attempt at relief from the pain I was experiencing. The chemicals completed the destruction of all my relationships not only with family but also friends, employers, and institutions. I became emotionally violent, passing hateful judgments on individuals and the entire culture in which I lived. I used arrogance and intimidation, backed up with the occasional burst of physical violence to get my way, to grab some power from experiences of powerlessness.[5]

I see an interconnectedness between the emotional processes of our collective humanity over a period of several years and that of individuals on a daily basis. My recovery from fear and distrust has helped me to see how out-of-control extremes of abusive human behavior, including my own rage at the micro level and national acts of war at the macro level, are part of normal, predictable learning patterns that can lead to stability and security, but only when there is new information, hope and mutual support available.

As a species, we are spread out around the bottom of the crisis as we approach the end of a long era of addiction to violence and domination. We are struggling with the multiple crises of environmental, energy, and economic changes, all of which trigger our addictions, including our addiction to aggressive thoughts, words, and deeds. Some of us on certain days feel that we are racing toward the edge of a cliff, exactly as addicts will do in the final stages of their addiction. At this point there is much alarm and protest as the abyss of chaos and the unknown fills the field of vision. Guilt is loudly denied as we look for someone to blame, and there is a sharp increase in verbal and physical abuse. Keeping the system in control still seems possible, but it is an illusion. We deny disaster is imminent with rationalizations of the most outrageous sort. Does this sound familiar, like the daily news?

On other days we may be feeling at our bottom or our emotions, completely disoriented, powerless and under tremendous pressure. Nothing works anymore. We feel completely lost. There is no hope, no trust. We are in free fall, enveloped in darkness, very sad and depressed. If you look at a display of 115,000 flags for the Iraq war dead, if you think about how many nuclear weapons are on hair-trigger alert, if you worry about abducted and missing children, or the extinction of polar bears, for more than a minute or two, then you will probably feel the feelings of being at this bottom. Intense anger, grief and even hyperventilation would be entirely normal at this point. It is a crisis, a very big crisis with a very uncertain outcome. This is where being born and dying have a great similarity! To be "born again" requires surrendering our ego, experiencing an ego death. If we avoid the intensity of this experience, we contribute to the repetition of the cycle of violence and we remain spiritually "unborn," a dilettante who talks the talk yet cannot walk the walk.

Learning to grieve

Have you noticed that it is common practice to avoid the grief process in our culture? It is actually a sign of health to participate in the process of letting go, to get ready for a change, and to welcome the rebirth process. The first part of the grief process is denial, in which we become numb to our

---

[5] Cf. Ari Cowan's framework for describing and understanding violence at http://www.spiritridgeinstitute.net/pgs/par/core-01.html

feelings and our intuition. Perhaps you have heard Pink Floyd singing "I have become comfortably numb" in the movie, *"The Wall."* That wall is the one keeping us separate from our true selves. This denial has become a permanent part of life for many people who repeat the addictive cycle as they seek the comfort of something familiar. I will detail this cycle in the next chapter.

The second stage of grief, which they are politely avoiding, is anger and outrage. As an example, political protesters who are angry about social injustice have entered this part of the cycle, and may seem to remain in it for a long time. Although protest seems to be a constructive means to influence the process of change, it can become a constant cynical repeating of the original stress if it does not include forgiveness. If we believe that we are so unlike, so separated from, those who are doing us harm, then we will also tend to believe that they are unable to see our point of view and change their behavior. I have seen within the anti-war and pro-peace movements this constant, ineffective antagonism and cynicism about people engaged in the military, Congress, the media and corporations. The polarizing effect of labeling others only prolongs this angry stage of grief.

The third stage, which we seldom see in Western culture, is feeling the totality of the sadness for all that is being lost, losing control of our feelings and letting them pour out. Joanna Macy, in her *Work that Reconnects,*[6] gives people the opportunity to experience and share their innermost response to the present condition of our world. In our culture we need more safety and support for this kind of "disconnect" process which is extremely painful for those who have had no prior experience of it. The loss of control can be terrifying. It is exactly like being pushed off the edge of a cliff. It takes a great deal of ego

strength and the self-worth that we gain from our personal and family relationships, to take that leap. We have to believe that someone or something will show us how to fly. In this stage it is important to keep moving, keep flying, and not look down. Going through this terror, this free-fall of seeming to be out of control, allows people to unlock their frozen feelings and accept their role, their response-ability, their power for moving forward. This creates the freedom to integrate an entirely new lifestyle, during the final phase of grief.

When I was in treatment, I was told that processing grief was an important part of recovery. I wasn't willing to dive headlong into grief at that time because I feared the overwhelming loss of control that I associated with it. However, as I persisted with the 12-step program, my courage grew. The principles of the program helped me to allow grief to be present and move in its own time. Life handed me grief in those early recovery years. I had let go of my doubts about fatherhood, and Valerie became pregnant. It seemed that life was starting over again, and I was often feeling grateful. Then tragedy struck. The fetus died prematurely and I became entangled, stuck, in grief. I couldn't allow my feelings to flow. At a very deep level, I was clinging to the irrational thought that I was somehow responsible for this death, that I had contributed to it or deserved it.

About the same time, as part of my internship to be a treatment counselor, I conducted an intake interview with an older gentleman who was in late-stage alcoholism. He didn't have enough insurance coverage to allow him into inpatient treatment and the hospital care that goes with that, so he was placed into outpatient treatment. This meant that he had to de-tox on his own, at home. His withdrawal symptoms accelerated to the point where he could no longer tolerate them. He took his own

---

[6] http://www.joannamacy.net/theworkthatreconnects.html

life with a handgun. I had felt connected to his man and his story. I could identify with his agony. The tragedy of his suicide put my emotions into a downward tailspin.

My supervisor spent some time getting me to talk. I finally allowed myself to attempt a natural grieving process as a path to sanity. In the midst of that process, I saw my resistance to the experience of grief coming from my internal garbage bag of low self-esteem, cynicism, and isolation. I set those thoughts aside and became truly outraged and angry at the disease that had taken so many lives and destroyed the vitality of so many others. I began to shed responsibility for my disease and assume responsibility for my recovery.

During my sixth year I had the courage to go to a rebirthing counselor. There I grieved deeply for the fatherly love that I hadn't received from Daddy, finally forgiving and letting go of that part of my childhood. In the middle of my tears, I saw how he also had not received love as a child. Afterwards, I wrote a completely honest letter to Daddy, sharing with him my understanding of why and how I had become so angry at him, and how he probably felt frustrated with me. I sent it to the caretaker of the cemetery in Vermont where he was buried, and asked that the letter be burned on his grave.

Since that time, I have grieved the loss of our Siberian husky, McKenzie, and my mother. Each time, the grief process becomes more familiar and less difficult, and yet full of surprising lessons. I learned that anger, the first stage of grief, isn't always a dangerous emotion as it had been in my childhood. It had healing potential. Being angry at life's situations, being angry at God, just being angry at frustrations became more acceptable and less shameful. Allowing anger to express itself as tears instead of violence overcame the isolation I had been defending and replaced it with connection. I could begin to empathize with the experience of

loss, not only in the lives of other addicts, but also my own father's losses, my mother's, and even our dog's.

On the the facing page is a graph drawn from the work of Neila Campbell, a talented grief counselor. I assume that Neila was unaware of Laszlo's graph when she drew her "Phases of, and Responses to, a Transition." The striking similarity between the two drawings lends some validity to both. We are not as unique as individuals as we might like to believe. I am guessing that you can see the similarity here between an addict's story, a grief process, and a systems-theory description of evolution applied to an entire cultural system. They all have up and down cycles of increasing intensity, and a sudden "jump" to the next level.

Neila defined grief as *resistance to change*. In other words, change itself doesn't cause suffering, our resistance to change does. I was taught as a child to block both expressions of anger and sadness for the sake of being strong, virtuous or grown up. However, when the internal rule to not cry continued to block my ability to grieve, I became stuck in guilt and fear. I judged myself as wrong for being angry or sad. As those feelings built inside me, I saw myself as the most angry and most pitiful person on Earth. I adopted a strategy of altering this image with chemicals so that I could appear to be a functional part of adult society. At the same time, my inner child was screaming. As the contradictions between my outward appearance and my inner reality repeated in endless cycles, I became reactive and hyper-sensitive to every change. My life became all about me defending myself against blame and hurt.

Addicts can be accurately described as people who resist growing up, and who remain stuck in adolescent narcissism. In order to recover, an entire lifestyle and pattern of thinking about oneself must be left behind. Thus, recovery from addictive behavior is a grief process.

PHASES OF, AND RESPONSES TO, A TRANSITION

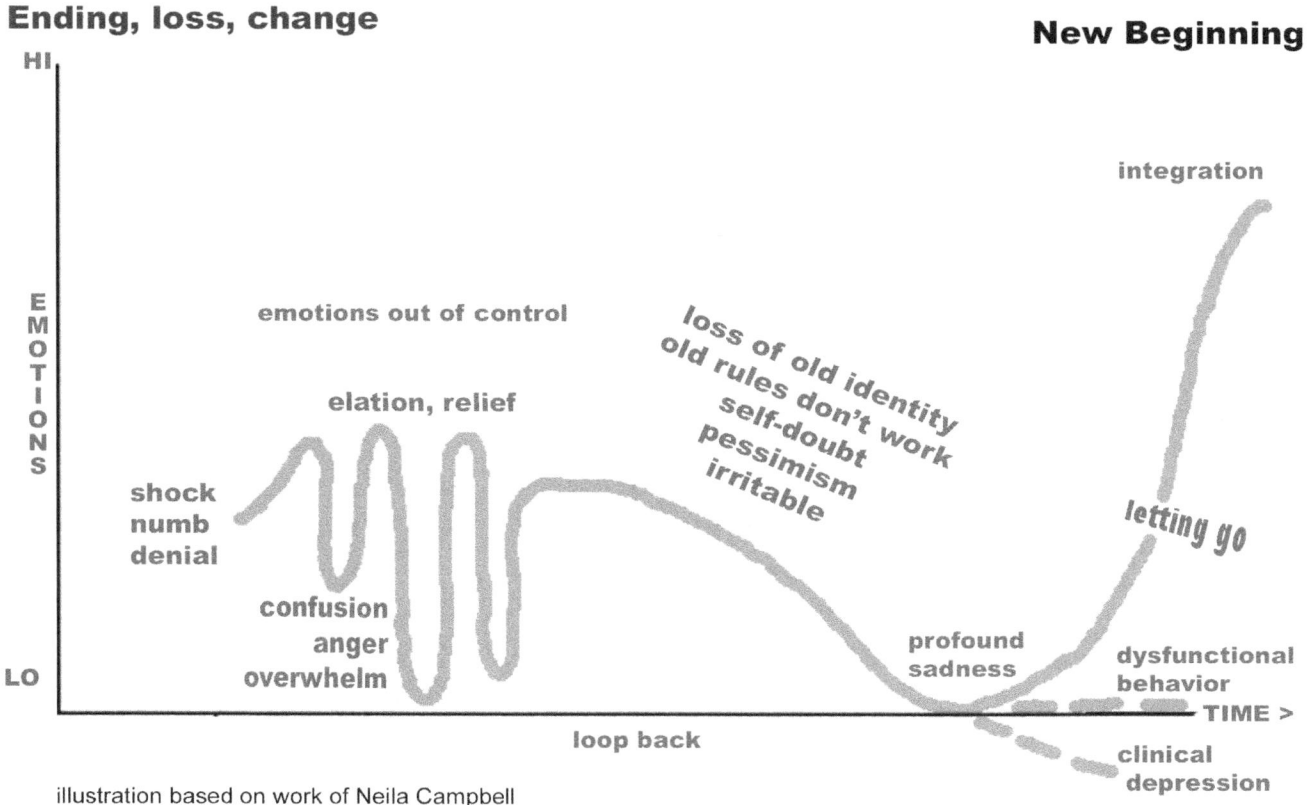

illustration based on work of Neila Campbell

In the first part of a grief process there are wide swings between elation and confusion. Releasing emotions feels incredibly healthy, and at the same time violates what we were taught about being responsible, stable, reliable individuals. We enter the second stage of grief when we realize that there is no going back to who we were. The relationship to a familiar person, place, object, lifestyle, or situation has finally been severed irrevocably. We feel ignorant and powerless about moving forward without that relationship. Feeling this vacuum plunges us into a profound and dark sadness which is completely normal. It is also our opportunity to rise toward a new world view. We can choose to cling to the past. That will bring us back to the emotional swings of the first stages of grief. This is not a healthy choice. Notice the position of "letting go." Letting go is a valuable life skill that only those who learn the lessons of grief seem to master. Hale Dwoskin has developed the Sedona Method to focus on the skill of letting go, and I recommend that you look for his DVD recordings as a valuable resource.

Empathy, hugs, safety, permission to fall apart, and patience are the best support interventions for helping a person to let go of their loss. This is the role that support groups can provide so that we can reach a state of self-forgiveness for being attached to what was lost, the old self-identity. It seems true that if we have lost touch with our emotional wisdom we have to hit bottom in order to find which way is up, have our hearts broken open repeatedly until they stay open. Perhaps in the crises now facing humanity we will be motivated to learn the lessons of grief. It will take some time, some practice, some real effort, and genuine courage to do what we have never done before.

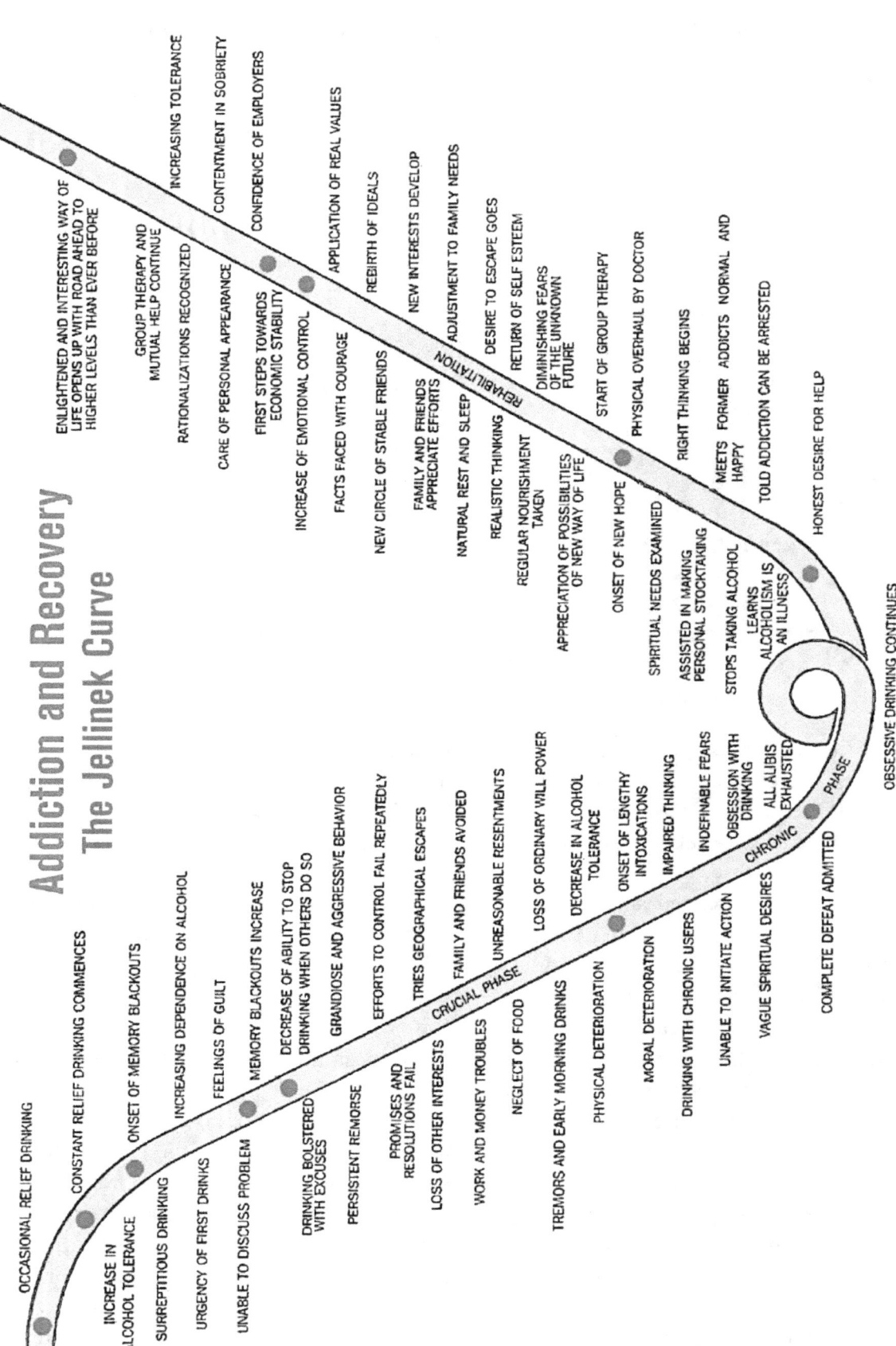

Addiction and Recovery
The Jellinek Curve

Addiction is a disease

Chemical dependency is considered a behavioral disease by most medical professionals. Treatment is based on the assumption that this disease affects not only the physical health of the individual but also their mental, emotional, and spiritual health. The whole person has been broken into parts that no longer work together as one system. When we frame it this way, we realize:

1. We can treat it, remission is possible,
2. The disease is separate from the individual,
3. It is no longer a moral issue, and
4. We have compassion for the individual, seeing their disease as a tragic failure to meet their own needs in functional ways.

On the opposite page, the Jellinek Chart displays the progression of the symptoms of alcoholism through the early, late, and recovery phases. The so-called "Jellinek curve" is derived from the alcoholism classifications of E. M. Jellinek, and it was named out of respect for his work.[7] Although Jellinek later completely dissociated himself from this chart's representations, it is still known as the "Jellinek curve." To me, this is a zoomed-in, detailed view of Laszlo's graph of transformation. We see here the cascade of crises, the falling into a hole, and the surge to a new level of functioning.

Alcoholism and other addictions can be viewed as a transformation opportunity in the midst of a much longer journey. It is important for us to analyze how this process begins and ends, as well as place it within the perspective of events leading up to and following the active disease which is represented by the Jellinek curve. The struggles of my childhood are not only the precursors to the final crises of my addiction, they are part of it. Although I no longer have to deal with repeating crises, the struggle to adapt to changing situations continues to this day in recovery. I may always be vulnerable to momentary self-doubts, behavioral slips, and failure. However, my overall health, stability, and creativity continues to grow.

Even though this curve was based on an analysis of alcoholism, most of the specific details can be generalized to other addictions by simple substitution of other behaviors for "drinking." Alcohol dependency is just one subset of many types of chemical dependency, which includes multiple categories of mood-altering substances from heroin and marijuana to nicotine. In addition, "mood-altering" can include not only other substances that we commonly ingest such as meat, caffeine and sugar, but also behaviors such as gambling, sex, shopping, and violence. The disease process of gradual descent into a helpless obsession with the substance or behavior, however, is the same process for all addictions.

Treatment professionals will tell you that addictions can be put into remission, but are never fully cured. The memory of an individual's favored coping mechanism, be it substance or behavior, is never lost and will return in stressful situations.

In my third year of recovery, I entered an intensive, year-long education as an intern counselor in a treatment program. I learned a great deal about the process of addiction and recovery, and found it helpful for me to summarize it this way:

Chemical Dependency (alcoholism and drug addiction) is the compulsively repeated alteration of brain chemistry by means of a toxin in order to produce temporary relief from frustration, grief,

---

[7] Jellinek, E. M., The Disease Concept of Alcoholism, Hillhouse, New Haven, 1960.

Addictive Behavior Cycle

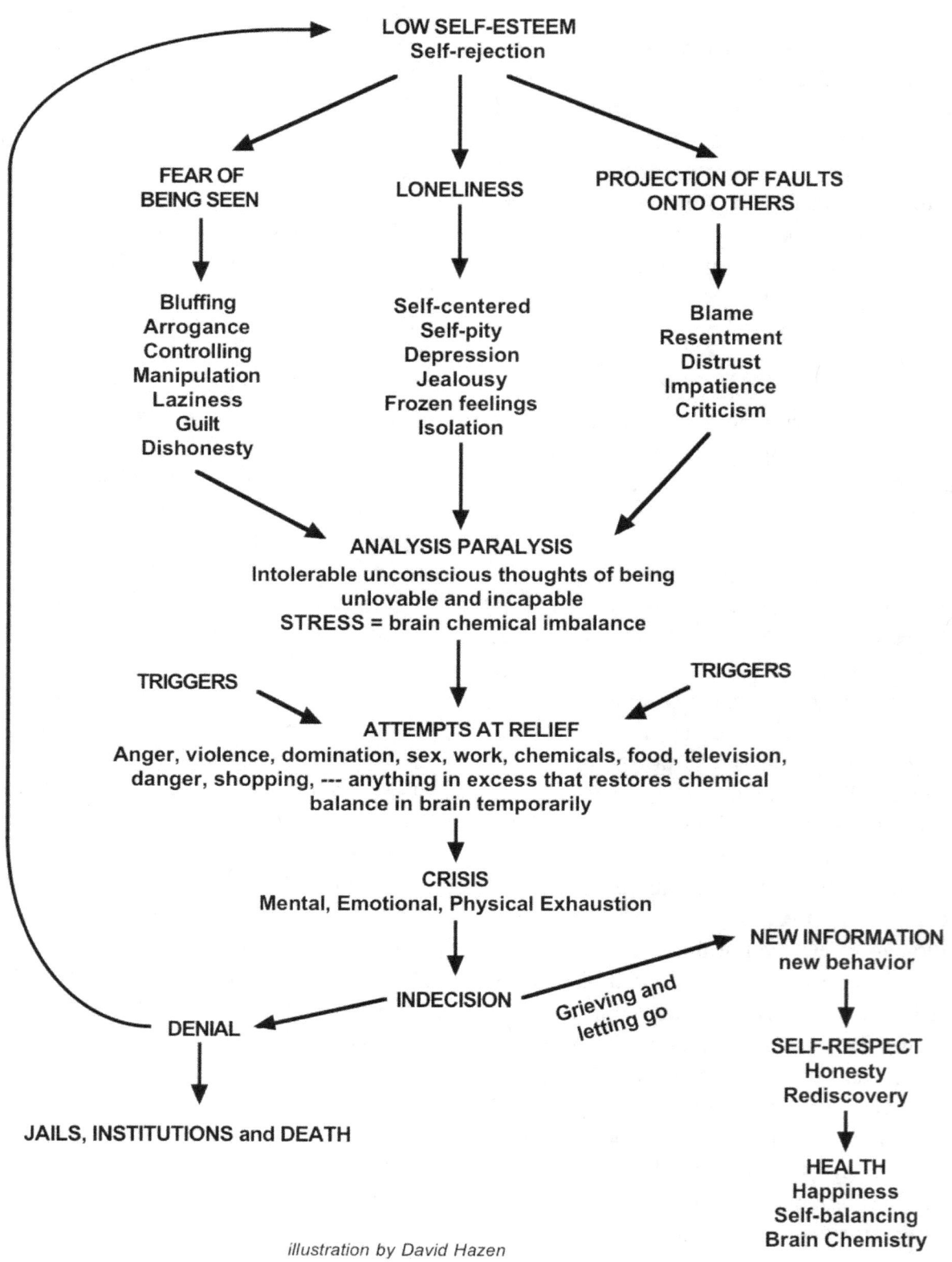

illustration by David Hazen

fear, or pain quickly without changing the thoughts or behavior that cause these negative feelings.

Chemical dependency is a treatable disease that can be held in remission through a basic lifestyle change. There is no known cure. The tendency to relapse is always present. The degree of dependency on chemicals always increases, even when the person is not using. If allowed to progress, the disease is fatal. Chemically dependent people typically have low self-esteem, poor coping skills, poor social skills, and come from abusive, chemically dependent, and dysfunctional family systems. They appear to be bored, confused, lonely, depressed, and angry. Although they feel guilty about their loss of control over their using and their behavior, thoughts, and feelings, they tend to blame others or external circumstances, and deny that they have a problem.

Treatment for chemical dependency educates the person that it is their biochemical reaction to the toxins which causes the loss of control, similar to an allergy. Emphasis is placed on rebuilding self-esteem, increasing awareness of feelings, and making lifestyle changes to obtain a more lasting and more satisfying happiness without chemicals. The most important message of treatment is the comfort and safety felt within a group of people who share in the same struggle.

In my recovery, I discovered that I have in common with other addicts a decision to trust no one. This goes hand-in-hand with low self-esteem, or lack of trust for oneself, and isolation. It is the classic victim position in which power is projected onto something or someone external

that becomes the "enemy." This is the baseline self-fulfilling prophecy that I used to set myself up for using chemicals, sex, food, work -- and violence -- to numb this pain of my utter isolation from other people. These addictive behaviors in me became "suicide on the installment plan," a long series of violations of my basic humanity, of violence against myself, creating layer after layer of toxic shame and guilt. These violations are a common thread in the story of every addict. They describe the progression of the disease not only in individuals, but also in an entire culture, as I will show you.

The diagram of the addictive cycle on the opposite page is based on self-observation of my own tendencies to revert to addictive behaviors when I am in a stressful situation. The "escape route" to new information and behaviors at the bottom right is the beginning of the recovery behavior cycle, which I will describe in the next chapter. It is the increasing intensity of the addiction cycle that produces what Jellinek saw as a plunge into ever-deeper levels of crisis. Notice that the entire cycle is rooted in low self-esteem, otherwise known as a "disease of the spirit."

The underlying purpose of any addiction is to restore stability and balance to a damaged self-concept. This self-disrespect, or self-rejection, leads to an exaggerated sense of inferiority or superiority. However, the temporary solutions to the fears, loneliness, and focus on other people's behavior have self-destructive long-term consequences. The basic needs for improved self-esteem and self-management skills are not met.

When the thoughts of being unlovable and inadequate become intolerable it is quite human to seek an expedient form of relief. External situations are perceived to be the agent of our misery, and so they act as triggers for addictive behavior reactions. It doesn't matter if it is chemicals, overwork, overspending, overeating, or over-indulgence in emotions such as anger, the precursor to violence. It is all part of the same addictive cycle.

The addictive behaviors feel good because they temporarily get a person out of their head, out of their mind, out of their intolerable fears around situations that seem to be out of control, and back into some reassurance that everything -- especially themselves -- will be OK. This is an important point, because this is what all addiction does. It is a strategy for getting out of one's rational, analytical thought process, for becoming more body aware, more emotionally aware, sometimes more spiritually aware. Any addict is, deep in their heart, a seeker of wisdom, truth and love. They are also sick with a behavior that continuously moves them further away from those things. All the energy and effort spent on conquering fear only makes their fear worse.

The mental, emotional, and physical exhaustion at the bottom is a kind of spiritual death, a crossroads where our inner voice is likely to say to us, "Give it up, quit, surrender. There must be a different way to live." If we actually follow this voice, and *grieve* the loss of our familiar strategies for being in control, we become open to discovering new behavior, new self-respect, and new well-being.

However, new or different behavior can also feel terrifying because it is unfamiliar and outside our ability to imagine it. Nothing is more frightening than the unknown. This is what keeps the cycle going. The reaction to fear is usually denial, in all its many forms: lying, rationalization, justification, minimization, and blaming others. When we are in denial, we are expressing our preference to live with the familiar, known, and predictable situations, even when they are quite ugly. This behavior runs at cross-purposes with the general welfare of society. In cases of overt injury to ourselves or others, we may be restrained by society in an institution, or we may die. We may run out of hope, and commit suicide as a form of self-restraint.

Violence is an addiction

I invite you to now look at aggressive, violent behavior as an addictive disease that affects the overall health of individuals and their community. Consider that humans might become dependent upon aggression-produced brain chemistry in the same way that they become dependent on drugs. These behaviors are not innate, [8]they are strategies, learned mostly from a culture of violence that is a public health epidemic.[9] We are all to some degree in need of recovery.

On November 7, 2008, a news article titled *Bullies Enjoy Being Mean*[10] described a scientific study of brain activity of aggressive children watching videos of someone inflicting pain on another person. "Aggressive adolescents showed a specific and very strong activation of the amygdala and ventral striatum — an area of the brain that responds to feeling rewarded — when watching pain inflicted on others, which suggested that they enjoyed watching pain," said Benjamin Lahey of the University of Chicago, who worked on the study. In situations that would normally provoke empathy, these children displayed symptoms of what the

---

[8] www.unesco.org/cpp/uk/declarations/seville.pdf

[9] Cohen, L. & Swift, S., A Public Health Approach to the Violence Epidemic in the United States in Environment and Urbanization (October 1993;5:50-66)

[10] http://health.usnews.com/health-news/family-health/brain-and-behavior/articles/2008/11/07/brain-scans-show-bullies-enjoy-others-pain

researchers at the University of Chicago termed "disruptive behavior disorder." The aggressive children repeatedly stole, damaged property or started fights.

Is this behavior really any different from what a nation does when it supports false placement of blame onto other nations, initiates devastating bombing campaigns against them and steals their resources?

The unspoken message of violence is "Get away from me, I cannot tolerate your presence, I cannot communicate with you, I am not in community with you, you do not belong to me." It is a message of extreme distrust that justifies any means necessary to control and dominate other people. It is a denial of connection based on F.E.A.R., which we use in the 12-step program as an acronym for False Evidence Appearing Real.

False evidence can include thoughts such as those about a potential enemy harboring weapons of mass destruction. It is based on the thought that we have been abandoned, that we are alone. From my own experience, I know that underneath my feelings of isolation is the mistaken belief that I am unable to attract the kind of support and connection that I most urgently desire. I believed that I was unlovable, defective, weak, and imperfect. As a child I didn't learn how to communicate my feelings of fear and grief. Instead, I learned how to manipulate, bully, and bluff so that I could judge myself to be strong, superior and in control.

I believe violence is caused in the same way as any addiction is caused. We overuse analytical, rational thinking about gaining control and power, and deny vulnerability to hurt or pain. These thoughts separate people from each other and produce situations of winners and losers. Violence repeats in cycles exactly like an addiction. These cycles block evolution, change or growth. Instead, they produce destructive changes and increasing chaos.

I now define violence very broadly, as any behavior of domination. The World Health Organization, in its first *World Report on Violence and Health,* defined violence as "the intentional use of physical force or power, threatened or actual, against oneself, another person or against a group or community, that either results in or has a high likelihood of resulting in injury, death, psychological harm, maldevelopment or deprivation."[11] To me, then, violence can be spiritual, psychological, emotional, verbal or physical. In the end, violence is using other people as objects to affirm our own virtue and strength, in the same way that addicts use chemicals to overcome their fear and pain.

By simply substituting "violence" for "chemicals" in my definition for chemical dependency, I get a definition for violence dependency that seems to me to ring true. See what you think:

> *Violence Dependency (domination disorder) is the compulsively repeated alteration of brain chemistry through stress in order to produce temporary relief from frustration, grief, fear, or pain quickly without changing the thoughts or behavior that cause these negative feelings.*
>
> *Violence dependency is a treatable disease that can be held in remission through a basic lifestyle change. There is no known cure. The tendency to relapse is always present. The degree of dependency on violence always increases, even when the person is not acting out. If allowed to progress, the disease is fatal. Violence-dependent people typically have low self-esteem, poor coping skills, poor social skills, and come from abusive, violence-dependent,*

---

[11] Krug EG et al., eds. World Report on Violence and Health. Geneva, World Health Organization, 2002.

and dysfunctional family systems. They appear to be bored, confused, lonely, depressed, and angry. Although they feel guilty about their loss of control over their violent behavior, thoughts, and feelings, they tend to blame others or external circumstances, and deny that they have a problem.

Treatment for violence dependency educates the person about the causes for the loss of control. Emphasis is placed on rebuilding self-esteem, increasing awareness of feelings, and making lifestyle changes to obtain a more lasting and more satisfying happiness without violence. The most important message of treatment is the hope, comfort and safety felt within a group of people who share in the same struggle.

To summarize, domination and violence come essentially from an inner panic -- feeling abandoned, alone, and unsupported in a situation that appears to be out of control. The process of letting go of self-centered grasping for control always heals violence and creates bonding between people. Those bonds lead to win-win situations that are creative, evolutionary and, from a whole-systems perspective, efficient. This is the definition of non-violence and compassionate love. Learning to communicate in ways that build community resolves the panic.

We all -- *yes, ALL* -- have a shadow side that can empathize with the desire to dominate, and we all -- *yes, ALL* -- have the capability of responding with mature, disciplined compassion to it. We may not be the ones who made our culture of violence, we may believe that we do not even participate in it, and yet we are capable of undoing what has been done for centuries. Violence can be unlearned.

The recovery cycle

I believe a certain chain of events typically describes the process of building a peaceful culture, whether it is within a person, a family, a neighborhood, a nation or the entire planet. The Recovery Behavior Cycle, mapped on the page opposite, is one way to represent the process that is initiated when a person or a culture chooses to let go of their addictive behaviors. This is an expansion of the lower right corner of the Addiction Cycle and a summary of the sequence of psychological processes that occur in a transformation of culture. The cluster of processes may occur simultaneously or loop backwards. There is no strict cause-and-effect implied by the direction or placement of the arrows, but a general indication of the flow.

In general, then, a crisis can create the pressure to admit there is a problem to which we have no answer, which leads to a willingness to listen. This is an initial act of surrender, which progressively deepens as the process continues. With the support of peers and mentors, a healthy dialog about our own behavior begins so that we can see how we contributed unwittingly to the crisis. Blaming others or ourselves (perfectionism) is seen as a distraction from the core issue of building trust and intimacy. The idea that we are victims loses its power. We no longer need to be vigilant about defending ourselves with grandiose notions of superiority or inferiority. We accept ourselves just the way that we are, both capable of mistakes and lovable. We begin to see other people in the same way.

Many layers of old habitual behaviors and thought patterns are eventually seen as dysfunctional. We adopt new behaviors, begin to respect collective wisdom, and see ourselves as part of a much larger systemic process. We feel

Recovery Behavior Cycle

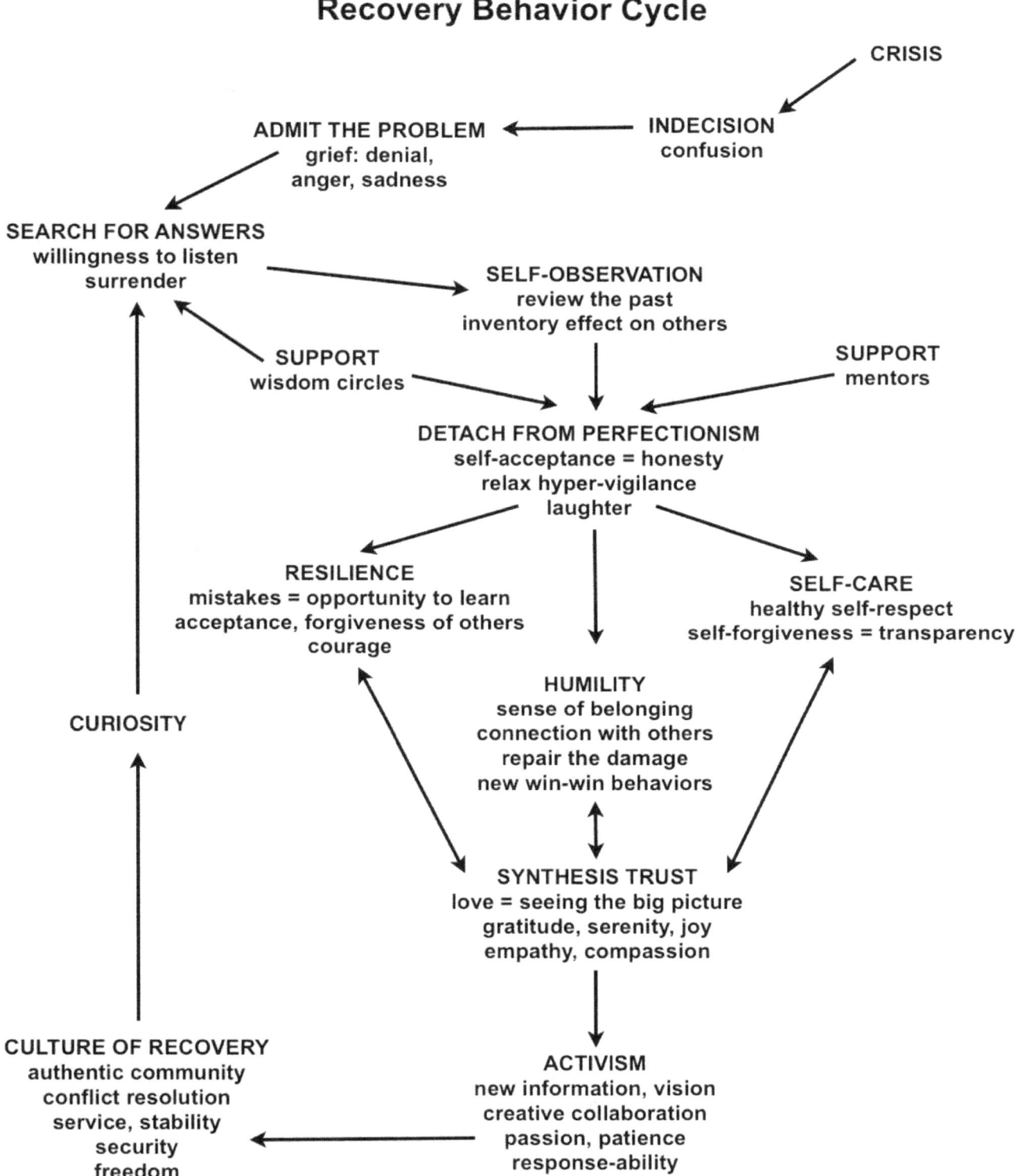

illustration by David Hazen

supported by, and trust, the hidden or spiritual process of our life. Our surrender to that process generates strong feelings of being loved. We no longer feel isolated and we are tremendously encouraged to collaborate in resolving social inequality. The new set of behaviors and attitudes, the culture of recovery, accelerates progress toward a sustainable, secure, prosperous and peaceful world. As we begin to build a world that works for everyone, we approach new problems with open, playful and creative curiosity.

I am encouraged by public conversations about sustainability and resilience in the last few years. Economic, energy and environmental problems are now being seen as global in nature. It is easy to say "We are all in this together" or "We are one." However, slogans cannot replace the searing self-examination and self-exposure -- the hard work -- involved in transforming our culture of addictive violence into a culture of peace. There are sweeping implications and deep difficulties involved in becoming one planet, one humanity, with one future. The scale of this transformation requires a social engineering effort comparable to the multiple corporations and thousands of teams involved in the project of sending a man to the moon, only with *many more* engineers and participants.

Living from the listener

Radical, active committed listening is the fuel that launches the recovery process. In the 12-step program, there is a structure of simple expectations for listening. Only one person speaks at a time, everybody is given enough time to finish what they need to say, and we don't comment on what other people said. We speak only about our own experience. We don't gossip, or at least we *try* to not gossip. This practice supports the anonymity of the members of the group, the confidentiality and safety of the group. What is said in meetings stays in meetings. It is now very exciting for me when I meet a real Listener outside of a 12-step meeting. Think about it, and it's probably true for you also. Do *you* need to be heard, *completely heard* in a safe situation?

The listener and the speaker are faced with the exact same question: "How much do I want to be really seen and known as I truly am?" The speaker is just telling their story, but the listener becomes just as visibly known by how well they listen, accept, and respect the story of another without comment, interpretation or expansion.

Listening -- not just hearing -- real listening is an act of love. When I am speaking, and an individual or group of people is listening to me with their full attention, not interrupting, and making eye contact with me, I can feel the acceptance. I can feel the love, and can trust that I am OK just the way I am. It's very difficult to perpetuate my distrust of others when I am constantly exposed to this kind of listening week after week in my 12-step meetings, and yet I have found myself threatened by it.

Some of us grew up with so many conditions laid upon us that we do not know how to respond to a lack of conditions. We may feel disoriented and lost. We truly are lost. We have lost our true selves. In spite of our desperately wanting to no longer live in the hell of solitary confinement, when the jail cell opens we duck for cover. We stop telling the truth about ourselves. We want to be loved unconditionally, to be trusted. We want to be truly safe, to be OK with not having the answers, and when this precious jewel of mutual trust and respect begins to appear, we are often too frightened to tell ourselves what it is we really need to hear.

The soul is like a wild animal: tough, resilient, savvy, self-sufficient, yet exceedingly shy. To see a wild animal, the last thing we should do is crash through the woods, shouting for the creature to come out. But if we walk quietly into the woods and sit silently for an hour or two at the foot of a tree, the creature may well emerge, and out of the corner of an eye we will glimpse the precious wildness we seek.[12]

Therefore, it is important as listener to allow speakers the time and space to find themselves in their speaking, to not help them out of their cocoon, to let them develop their own conclusions, lessons and meanings to their own life story. We cannot force someone else to be honest or to say more than they want to say. We cannot make them accept our analysis and interpretation of their situation. We cannot solve their problems or reveal what they should do next in their life.

As listener, we need to "just drive the car that we are in," and not someone else's. Our analyzing another person could be a way of avoiding being seen, of hiding, of keeping the focus away from what we fear, the emptiness within us that seems so real (it isn't).

This kind of listening is done with humility. Humility is the awareness that regardless of what role or title we have borne in human society, we are but a speck of sand on the beach of the Universe. We are equal to all the other grains of sand, yet still have a unique role in the unfolding of the Universe.

When we respect another's privacy, their sense of living within their own skin, their boundaries and limits that protect them from being used, controlled or invaded by another person, that respect develops trust between us.

That trust encourages openness. Deep within a person who speaks openly we begin to see our essential selves, and we hear the echo of our own story within their story.

Our work in the cultural recovery from violence dependency is on ourselves. It takes more courage and strength of character to trust our angry and grieved companions on this journey, to stay in communication, than it does to imagine that we have the answer. We cannot claim to have "the answer," because we don't know what it really is. All we have is a crude map. There are many paths that all lead to the same place.

Listening to others is a form of service to them. As we develop skill in that service, we begin to also develop the ability to listen to our own deepest internal self-talk. We develop a compassionate witness, a self-empathy and self-respect. We see the similarity between the stories we tell ourselves and the stories we are hearing. The irony of our mutual foolishness begins to emerge in bursts of laughter and sometimes in bursts of shared tears. This is what I see happening in 12-step recovery meetings.

Eventually, as shared insights become the things that we treasure, we discover something unexpected and unpredictable will arise, especially if more than two people are present. In small groups that are gathered in circles expressing the equality of all those present, a wisdom beyond the capacity of any one person will bubble to the surface, literally pop out of someone's mouth without any forethought. This has been known in indigenous cultures since the dawn of humanity and lost in the industrialized culture. When given the space to be there, a collective wisdom, a creative solution to a vexing problem, appears spontaneously out of seemingly nowhere.[13]

---

[12] Palmer, Parker J., Contemplative by Catastrophe, Spirituality & Health, Spring 2002

[13] Briskin, A., et al, The Power of Collective Wisdom, Berrett-Koehler, San Francisco, 2009

There are currently many cutting-edge practitioners developing ways to apply this phenomenon not only to personal development but also to organizational development in business and politics.[14]

To summarize, I suggest that listening is the primary activity for building a culture of peace, within a person, a family, a neighborhood, a nation or the entire planet. If we practice deep listening, we begin to live according to these four principles:

1. We release all expectations. The less fixed our ideas about what peace is supposed to look like, or how to get there or how soon, the more able we will be to recognize resources as they arise. This is a multi-year experiment, one step at a time, and may require restarting the process several times.

2. We regard everyone as a resource, because everyone in our life is a stakeholder, and no matter their level of involvement, they each have a unique contribution to make. Peace is about inclusiveness.

3. We focus on the process, not the result. In order to empower ourselves to take action, we need to create connection that is heart-to-heart, face-to-face, and to allow an abundance of time and space for conversation to occur. We encourage listening and empathy skills. We build the common story of what's valued.

4. We see ourselves as part of a movement that focuses on strengthening positive assets. We're not on a campaign to force specific changes to happen. We avoid fixed positions, declarations, becoming institutionalized, or issue-focused. This is

about maintaining a conversation, a vision and hope of what is possible, not about policies or politics.

---

[14] http://ncdd.org/rc/best-of-the-best-resources

Steps to peace

The question that I had to answer in my early recovery was whether or not I was willing to be in community with others, and beyond that, in communion with a higher power. Being in community now means to me a willingness to work together, to collaborate.

Back then, I could not see that we have been freely given many collaborations. The very atoms and molecules of the entire physical world are collaborations, held together, interacting together, working together in an incredible continuous process that seems to have an orderly purpose and direction. Our bodies are living collaborations of billions of individual cells, living symphonies of incredible passion, always birthing, always dying in a constant process of renewal. The "spirit" of collaboration pervades all that is. So for me, God, Higher Power or whatever name you prefer to use for this great mystery, is a collaboration, meaning literally anything that can be seen as co-labor, a "working together."

I know from experience that I cannot be self-centered and participate in a collaboration. I must surrender my ego, my vanity and most of all, my distrust. I must acknowledge and release my self-centeredness. This is the key to not only personal recovery but also the cultural recovery from a dependency on control, domination and violence. A culture of peace is a culture of collaboration.

"I am a peacemaker: I conceive endless ways to collaborate and to spread reciprocal benefit." – Mali Rowan

I believe the truth is we are *all* in community all the time, no matter what our belief or preference has become. To say otherwise is a lie. Our illusion of separation from "those other people" is only a reflection of our own inner separation from our true, objective identity. We have the resources within us to communicate effectively without violence. Most of us simply haven't uncovered, discovered, or recovered those abilities.

In this book, I tell the story of my recovery. My readers have consistently told me that my story is the most relevant and interesting material in this book. I've been a bit shy about full self-disclosure. It felt like a kind of nakedness. Now I realize my story is the main thing I have to share. So is your story! As with personal stories shared in support groups, I hope my story will make abstract notions tangible, measurable, and listener-friendly.

My recovery has been guided by the twelve-step program for recovery established by Bill Wilson and Doctor Bob in 1935, for Alcoholics Anonymous. Those steps have been adapted since then into many other anonymous fellowships, all of which are focused on a specific type of addiction, be it food, work, sex, drugs, gambling, shopping or care-taking others. I have attended meetings in several different twelve-step fellowships, and the wording of the steps varies only slightly, to address the specific kind of addiction in the room.

Throughout the remainder of this book, I will primarily be talking about my addiction to control, domination, and violence. Even though my initial presenting symptoms indicated a diagnosis of chemical dependency in 1985, my understanding today is that those chemicals were being used to numb the pain of the underlying violence in my life. The chemical dependency was only accelerating my loss of control over that violence. In the chapter "Admit the Problem," I tell the story of how I defended my sense of security by dependence on various forms of violence that increased in intensity over time.

As far as I know, there has not been a fellowship created for recovery from violence dependency specifically, perhaps because violence is a common pattern within every addiction. However, the violence epidemic we are now experiencing in our families, communities, media, schools, prisons, departments of government and international relations may indicate the time has come for a recovery movement for violence. I was very pleased to discover Mark Umbreit has written the *Twelve Steps of Personal Peacemaking* that could be used for just such a movement. I present them here as simply a suggested guide for the work of personal transformation in combination with self-disclosure in a safe group environment.

The twelve-step meetings have been referred to as support groups for good reason. In those meetings we share our personal stories with each other, pooling our experience, strength, and hopes. The talking is our opportunity to practice communication skills we may have never learned in our childhood. Over time, we build healthy relationships within this community, and generalize on what we've learned to extend our community out into the world.

Not all of us have the inner tyrant that would make us unlovable and incapable of love, but I don't think you would be reading this book if the title weren't somehow challenging or provocative to you. With the support of a higher power, a group of companions, a mentor and much self-reflection and practice, we can learn to have satisfying, creative relationships. We can learn to love. We can trust that others really love us. To someone like myself, this is nothing short of magic and miracles.

The 12 steps are an effective framework that focuses our attention on what to talk about. They are the background on which we co-create self-forgiveness for our mistakes. We make mistakes, sometimes very harmful, violent mistakes. However, we ourselves, our lives are not mistakes. We need to know who we are and to love ourselves enough to be able to learn from and let go of our mistakes. We can learn from our mistakes instead of identifying with them. We can separate who we are from our behavior. Then the mistakes become our steppingstones to freedom from that tyrant voice within us.

The traditional Twelve Steps have always referred to God as the higher power, and referred to him only in the masculine gender, which was acceptable mainstream language in 1935, when those steps were first written. The more recent steps by Mark Umbreit have a more modern and inclusive re-wording of the original 12 steps while maintaining their essential intent. God can be known by any name, gender, or concept that symbolizes that energy.

Other changes were made to enhance their relevance to a culture of violence. For example, in Step One, the traditional version would simply say that whatever the particular addiction was, it had made life "unmanageable." Umbreit expanded that to say conflict and violence is consuming too much energy, creating stress and leading to unhappiness. Those words help to define unmanageability.

Those of us familiar with the original Twelve Steps may appreciate Umbreit's application of them to conflict and violence. In succeeding chapters, I will illustrate how they apply to my personal recovery.

Twelve Steps of Personal Peacemaking[15]

These steps are a modified version of the internationally embraced Twelve Steps of AA. They are reprinted here by permission of the author, Mark Umbreit, Director of the Center for

---

[15] http://www.cehd.umn.edu/ssw/RJP/Resources/Forgiveness/TwelveSteps.pdf

Restorative Justice & Peacemaking at the University of Minnesota.

1. *Admit that conflict and violence within yourself and among your relationships consumes too much of your energy, creates stress, and leads to unhappiness.*

2. *Believe that a power greater than yourself can bring you strength and peace.*

3. *Make a commitment to connect with a higher power, as you understand it, whether this higher power be understood as [the collective wisdom of a group], God, Yahweh, Allah, Buddha, Krishna, Mother Earth-Father Sky, The Divine, or whatever understanding brings you strength and peace.*

4. *Make an honest moral inventory of how you have contributed to conflict and violence in your personal relationships, your life in community, and as a citizen of your country and the world. Accept the fact that often your best intentions result in unintended negative consequences upon other people.*

5. *Admit to your higher power, to yourself, and to others the exact nature of your contributions to conflict and to emotional or physical violence.*

6. *Focus more on the here and now. Slow down. Breathe deeply. Keep life and your conflicts in perspective. Become responsible for your feelings and behavior.*

7. *In a spirit of humility and compassion for yourself and all others, seek spiritual guidance in confronting your shortcomings which may contribute to conflict and emotional or physical violence.*

8. *Make a list of all persons you have harmed and become willing to make direct amends to all such people wherever possible, except when to do so would injure them or others.*

9. *Continue to be mindful of your actions and their effect on others, and when you have offended another, whether intentionally or not, promptly admit it and apologize.*

10. *Seek through prayer, meditation, and other self-care techniques, to gain emotional and spiritual strength (in the context of your specific religious or secular tradition).*

11. *Forgive those who may have offended you. Don't take things too personally. Remember that most people don't mean to offend, but that their actions (and yours) frequently lead to unintended negative consequences.*

12. *Commit to being an instrument of peace and healing among all those who cross your path in your life's journey. Don't hang onto resentment and anger. Let it go. Remember, the one who benefits the most from forgiveness is the person who gives it. It can bring a renewed sense of freedom and energy to your life.*

These steps are not simple platitudes, they are the meme for an entirely new lifestyle. Changing personal habits cannot be done with impatience or superficial effort. The process of self-examination and reflection is best done in the context of daily life where small encounters provide opportunities for practicing new skills. Becoming ready to move on to the next step is a deliberate and respectful process. Each of these steps builds on the work done in the previous step. It defeats the whole process of personal transformation if we skip ahead.

The next several chapters will examine how my personal life was slowly but permanently affected by 12-step recovery. I am not suggesting that the 12-step program is the only way to recover from violence dependency, or that it is appropriate for everyone. I am simply sharing what works for me. There are many wisdom traditions, some of them religious, some of them philosophical or rational-scientific, and yet I believe they all lead to the same place, a renewed sense of freedom and energy. So take what you like and leave the rest.

If you should choose to work these steps, you may want to get a copy of a workbook-style, detailed guide to each step, *"The 12 Steps -- A Way Out."*[16] It is also helpful to have a small weekly discussion group of friends for keeping each other encouraged and accountable for working each step. Before you do that, you will probably want to know what it took for me to work these steps and what changes they made in my life.

---

[16] Friends in Recovery, The 12 Steps - A Way Out, RPI Publishing, 1995.

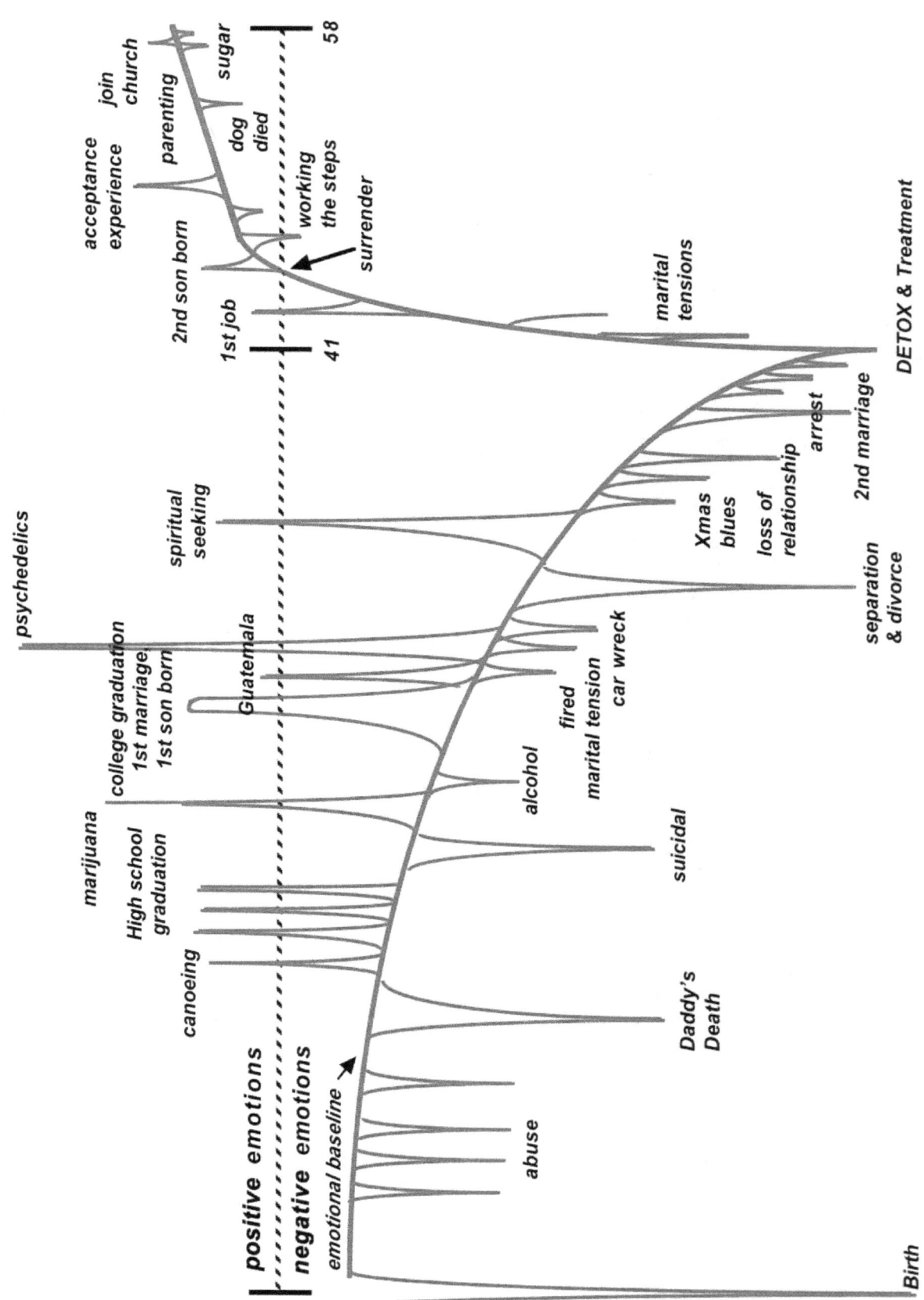

Step 1: Admit the problem

1. Admit that conflict and violence within yourself and among your relationships consumes too much of your energy, creates stress, and leads to unhappiness.

Admitting that I had a problem was the first step toward moving my disease into remission and releasing the toxic shame and guilt. In order for me to see the problem more clearly, I was asked by my treatment counselor to write a First Step, an autobiographical account of the childhood events leading up to my active use of chemicals and the history of that using and its effects on myself and others. My awareness of my addiction grew as I became willing to be more forthright and honest. I wrote another, more complete, First Step a few years later in preparation for becoming a treatment counselor. Fourteen years after treatment, when I repeated my story for new patients in treatment several times, I got to hear it again. I appreciated how much progress I had made in recovery and began to see more deeply into the trends of my disease. I began to visualize the ups and downs over time as a line on a graph. On the page opposite is that detailed graph of my emotional history, naming the peaks and valleys of my life. This is my personalized version of the more general Jellinek curve.

Now, after 26 years of recovery, I can see that the root cause of my addictions to chemicals, people-pleasing, perfection, work, control, domination, verbal and physical abuse is the loss of the secure, trusting part of myself that was so close to the surface when I was a child.

My Dad took the photograph above when I was 4 months old. It best expresses to me this essential part of myself. When I say I am recovering, it implies that part of the work, the

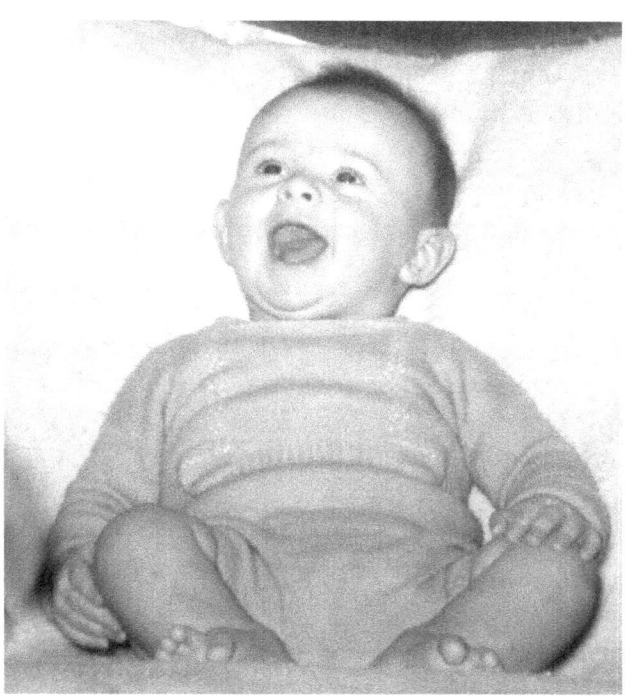

problem, the puzzle of recovery is to re-define and affirm the existence of this inner child. My First Step, then, is a grief-stricken story of loss.

My trip to hell

I definitely felt powerless at my birth. My first experience of life outside the womb was horrible. I was in a hurry to be born that November night in 1943, and the midwife kept telling my mother to not push until she could be wheeled into the delivery room. I was two weeks overdue, a large baby at 9 pounds, and painfully large for the small 120-pound frame of my mother. I was her third child.

My first shock was the cold air in the delivery room, then the doctor held me upside down and hit me two or three times to make me cry. I was outraged! I was taken away from Mother and put in a nursery so that she could recover from the anesthetics that had been injected into her bloodstream, and coincidentally into mine as well. My first drug experience was a painkiller.

My father was not present. He was working at his job as a civil engineer with a railroad in another state. He took his work very seriously and probably fit the diagnosis for workaholism.

I cried and cried for a very long time, calling for attention until I gave up. In that moment, I decided to not trust other human beings. I didn't recall this decision until perhaps 30 years later when I was struggling to discover why my life was such a mess. I underwent a hot water rebirthing process in the early 1970's and discovered these memories buried deep within my musculature. Perhaps they were so deep they were in my bones.

My father's father had a reputation for his rigid, authoritarian rule. He was probably a binge-drinking alcoholic. My Daddy was the youngest of his father's 7 children, and acquired the nickname "Nemo," which means "nobody" in Latin, so I am guessing Daddy's self-esteem was not very healthy. He carried forward the rigid, authoritarian traits of my grandfather without the alcohol. However, Daddy gunny-sacked his anger and exploded violently, unpredictably, just like an alcoholic. I became hyper-vigilant, observing his every nuance of mood, including the way that he walked. I could hear the sound of his footsteps like a voice speaking a telegram, "Watch out!" or "You're safe now."

In between explosions, I experienced intimidation and verbal abuse. At dinner he would often ask, "What did you do to earn your keep today?" as if I were a vassal to his kingship. If I were crying he would say, "Shut up or I will really give you something to cry about." I could not count on Mom to protect me. Instead, she would intimidate us kids with the threat of Daddy's heavy hand if I didn't obey her. If I talked back to Mom, I could be punished, slapped or whipped with a belt by Daddy. I was not allowed to explode in anger like he did. Anger was a taboo for us children,

so one day when nobody was watching, I released my anger physically. I took a sledge hammer and smashed all the flagstones in the path in Mom's flower garden. Later, Daddy lined up us three kids and demanded to know who had done it. We all froze in silent terror.

Many times Mom would remind us three children of what a burden we were to her, which was a form of psychological abuse. I vividly remember her telling me she wanted to strangle me. Mom had a hysterectomy after I was born, and I don't know the true reason for it, but my interpretation was that I was the unwanted child who pushed her stress level beyond what she could tolerate, so she was determined not to have any more children.

I became what is called in family systems therapy the classic "lost child." I spent most of my time playing alone. When I was upset, I would disappear and find my power in being noticed by my absence. Mom told me that when I was very little I would cross the road and go down to the river to play without telling her. She would get frantic, looking for me. When I was a little older, I once hid under the bed for six hours, listening to the sounds of my family calling my name, looking for me. On another occasion, I didn't say anything before I walked away from home for several hours. I can't remember how far I walked, and perhaps it was only a few miles. I probably wanted to simply cool my anger before I did something that would put me at risk of really getting hurt by Daddy. I also wanted to get some attention for being missed. Helpless and scared, I came home the same evening, unable to say what was bothering me. It wasn't OK to even feel sad or mad, so I became numb.

Toxic shame and self-pity took root in my heart and grew. In elementary school I was bullied by an insensitive teacher who held up my math paper for all the other students to see what I had done. Because I didn't understand the problems and made so many mistakes, I had drawn huge "X" marks from edge to edge of the paper with my ruler.

I didn't fit into the social scene at school. The other students quickly discovered that I was the kid who would explode, and they would tease and bully me until I was screaming and kicking. I even bit a kid, which only led to more shame in the principal's office. She told me "only girls bite." Another time, the kids in my neighborhood were teasing me, and in a murderous rage I grabbed my father's .22-caliber rifle out of a closet. I felt very powerful as I chased them down the street and they ran from me in terror. Fortunately, I didn't know anything about how to shoot a gun. Had I known, I could have been a youth homicide statistic long before the rate young people were killing each other in the USA rose to a peak. In 2002 the rate was *ten* times that of other industrialized countries.[17]

As I grew older, the family moved several times as Daddy changed jobs between different railroads, and I was repeatedly put in the situation of the newcomer and outsider at school. I never had a stable group of friends. At ten years of age, I was externalizing my fears into physical symptoms. I developed allergies, eczema, skin fungi, and severe intestinal cramps that put me in the hospital for examination. When I was released from the hospital, a doctor told my parents that I needed psychiatric therapy, advice that my parents ignored.

There were some good times. Daddy taught me how to ski, and how to work with tools to make intricate model airplanes and trains. He took us camping and on wonderful railroad trips out West to the national parks. I got to sing in the choir of a beautiful stone cathedral with an extremely talented choir director and pipe organist, an experience that was more deeply spiritual for me than I knew at the time. I never lacked for material things. I went to many years of summer camp and learned to love canoeing and the outdoor life. Daddy, a product of a college prep school himself, sent all of us kids to private prep schools and created a college trust fund.

However, the toxic shame was relentless, and I found ever more creative ways to keep it fed. When I was in fifth grade I became a pyromaniac, setting fire to trash in the basement fireplace of our home when nobody else was home. One day, while playing with fire in an old wooden bus shelter, it got out of control, and an entire field of dry grass went up in flames along with the bus shelter. This was the only time in my life that I heard Daddy cry. He was lying in bed, slowly dying of Hodgkin's disease and didn't have the strength to give me the usual whipping. I felt overwhelmed with shame. As his disease slowly took him down, the reason for "good behavior" was no longer to protect ourselves from the sting of his belt, it was to protect Daddy from disappointment and stress.

It wasn't too much longer after that when I proudly showed Daddy a funny question I had printed on a small printing press he had given to me for a Christmas present. My Latin teacher had asked this pun, "Time will pass, will you?" He meant would we all get passing grades in his class. However, when Daddy saw it, he said, "Yeah, pretty soon, son." My heart sank. He was mentally preparing to die. I was wracked with guilt for making such a blunder, convinced of my utter worthlessness and simultaneously wrestling with the fear of abandonment. It was the only time we had a conversation of any length about his death, and he never said another word about it, never said goodbye to me, as if my feelings about it were unimportant.

There was no conversation after he died, either. My grandfather simply told me to be strong for my mother. I was fourteen years old. I had stuffed incredibly strong feelings so deep I

---

[17] Krug, E.G. et al., eds. World Report on Violence and Health, World Health Organization, Geneva, 2002.

didn't know what they were. It wasn't until years later that I discovered in therapy that the thought that I held most secret was a wish to commit revenge on Daddy for all the abuse I had received. I had wished that he would die, I had wanted to kill him. The secondary feeling on top of that was the shame for having such a taboo wish and having it come true.

About this time in the mid-1950's the United States and Russia were having a nuclear arms race that generated widespread fear. Bomb shelters and emergency drills were a common form of cultural psychological abuse. I had nightmares of incineration by an atomic bomb. However, I saw that the hostility between nations was no different than Daddy's explosive anger, which was so much like a nuclear bomb. Somehow, I connected survival with learning how to communicate. I began to wonder about the mechanics of the human brain as the possible source of miscommunication, and later in college I studied perception and physiological psychology. However, the solutions weren't there.

I became more isolated within myself as I continued through high school, and even became proud of how self-reliant and non-conformist I had become. I wore red suede shoes to school in defiance of the preppie upperclassmen who wanted to beat me to a pulp for not modeling their conservative wing-tips and penny loafers. My senior yearbook profile refers to me as "phosphorescent" because of those bright red shoes, and accurately described my character as an eccentric visionary. After several years of YMCA summer canoe camp in northern Minnesota, I was employed as a canoe trip guide. I earned the nickname "Blazin' Hazen" because I would blaze new trails, crashing through the woods where there were no trails, to get to lakes on the map that nobody had seen.

I scored high on the scholastic aptitude tests, and was admitted to Dartmouth, the Ivy League college in New Hampshire where not only had my father graduated, but also his father, his brother, and many other of my male predecessors. I intended to be loyal to the family tradition and become a civil engineer, but those dreams were soon dashed.

The college was strictly for males (this was 1961), and I just didn't have the social skills to connect with anyone. I quickly responded to the intense academic pressure with melancholy and suicidal thoughts. After several attempts to resolve things with a counselor, I decided to run, just run, run away as far as I could go. I took my tuition money and bought a used car. Half-way home to Minneapolis, I phoned Mom to tell her I was on my way, and she said, "No, you're not!" in utter disbelief and denial that there could be anything that I couldn't solve on my own. Two days later I showed up, dazed and confused, looking for answers about what the hell I was doing on this crazy planet. In grade school, I had fantasized that I wasn't human. It made more sense to believe that I was an alien sent here to observe these strange humans, and that everything I had seen was being relayed back to my true home planet. This feeling of being an outsider contributed to my becoming, in reality, a very acute observer and in college I began developing a talent as a photographer.

Once I arrived back home, I began a life-and-death struggle with God. I tried to surrender to Jesus at a Billy Graham revival, and I couldn't bring myself to do it. I decided I was agnostic, and that wasn't good enough for me. I was desperate. I asked God to blind me as proof of his existence, to take the vision that I enjoyed so much from my life. Today I am grateful that he didn't do it. At the time, I decided to keep running. God was possibly out there somewhere, I thought, he just didn't give a damn about me, and if he did, I didn't want him to find me, anyway, because he might just do to me what Daddy would have done. I was trapped in the circle of my own fears. Shit!

I ran beyond home. I ran to the West coast, to San Francisco, where the car cracked its engine block, broke its heart, just as my own heart was breaking. For some strange reason, instead of giving in to my thoughts of suicide, I got into a phone booth and looked up a social worker who proceeded to save my life. Looking back at this event I feel tears of grief for all the lost opportunities for growth and development in my childhood. I realize if I had been looking for proof of the existence of God, it was right there in that "strange reason" inside of me when I picked up that phone to talk to someone about how hopeless I felt. However, God was to remain hidden from me for many more years.

That social worker I had called got me to move out of the YMCA, where I had been staying, and into a boarding house with other students. She convinced me to look for work in photography, and I started to get grounded. I got a job as a darkroom assistant. I began to wander the city with a new camera, joined a public darkroom, and literally bloomed into artistic creativity. I experienced some real happiness around my new-found independence.

Then my colleague in the darkroom offered me a joint. I can still remember the sensation of that first high, when I drank some orange juice and heard a roaring, gushing waterfall going down my throat. Words and feelings were also gushing out of me, and I felt a tremendous release from the emotional prison in which I was holding myself. I had discovered a tool for getting outside of myself, and for getting connected to other people. I was also naive about the side-effects of using this medicine.

Within a few months, Mom was telling me that I "owed myself an education," and I submitted to those guilty feelings. I came home and attended the nearby University of Minnesota. I enjoyed the co-ed classes and more access to photography and film courses. I entered long-term psycho-analysis to deal with my depression. Apparently the therapist became frustrated with my lack of progress one day and recommended that I "loosen up" by getting drunk. His suggestion represented the state of medical knowledge about addiction and alcoholism in 1962. I journeyed during spring break with some classmates far from home, away from Mom, to Florida where it was easy to purchase alcohol from a grocery store.

I knew nothing about what whiskey would do to me, but I thought it might "make a man out of me." I think I drank an entire pint in about 20 minutes and passed out shortly thereafter. If I didn't have a high tolerance for alcohol this could have stopped my heart. Instead, I was simply weak and nauseated for three days afterwards. I swore I would never do that again. Of course, I did. I indulged in binge-drinking of beer for the rest of my college years and later on returned to whiskey, gin and vodka as my tolerance for alcohol progressed.

By the time I finished college and grad school, I was no longer binge drinking, I was doing maintenance alcoholism, consuming 2 to 3 beers on 4 to 5 days per week. I had become an angry opponent of the Vietnam war, claiming but never gaining conscientious objector status, and marching on the Pentagon in 1967. I met a woman on that march with whom I became involved and infatuated. Little did I know that Barbara was an adult child of an alcoholic and would naturally be attracted to an alcoholic-addict like me. We were married about 8 months later, and my first son, Chris, was born in 1969.

My life slowly began a downhill slide into deeper chaos. I would find sources for marijuana from time to time, and began to add psychedelic drugs like LSD and mescaline into the mix. I lost two public school teaching jobs in a row for misbehavior on my part, once for being politically incorrect in my opposition to the war, and the second time for physically assaulting a student. Leading up to the assault, I had hidden my simmering anger until I exploded violently. I had become my own worst enemy.

I had become like my father, something I swore I would never do. I never used a belt like Daddy, and spanked Chris far fewer times than I had been spanked. Verbal abuse became my form of violence. I cultivated a piercing sarcasm with which to flay my child and anyone who crossed me. I teased my son about his crying, just like my father did to me. One day when my son was 5 years old, I goaded Chris into screaming, "I hate you!" That stopped me in my tracks. Chris was able to say out loud what I secretly wished I could have screamed at my own father.

After a second job loss, I felt alien to mainstream culture. I grew a beard, long hair, and became self-employed as a canoe builder. We moved three times in the next four years, finally landing at a farm-house with a barn in central Oregon, two hours drive from the nearest large city, Portland. I never saw how my increasing self-reliance and independence was coupled with greater isolation, arrogance, and self-centeredness. I drank beer every day and smoked pot several times a week. I withdrew further into myself, into my workshop, and became a workaholic like my father. I neglected my relationships with my wife and son. I neglected simple realities like the condition of the tires on the car. As a result, we skidded off the road at 60 miles per hour. The car rolled over, smashing all the windows. Fortunately, we were all in our seat belts and survived without physical injury. Psychologically, we were traumatized.

After 6 years of marriage, Barbara and Chris were both unhappy with the isolation of rural living as well as my depressed moodiness. They wanted to move to the city, I wanted to stay in the country. Our marital communication had devolved into superficial, intellectual competition. We did a Jungian Gestalt marathon weekend to work on our marriage. It was there that I imagined myself talking face-to-face with my father and screaming at him that I wanted to kill him. As disturbing as this was, and as much as it opened deeper conversation between myself and Barbara, the improvement in our relationship was short-lived.

Barbara took a trip to Los Angeles to visit her parents and wound up at Esalen. There she met some enthusiastic students of Oscar Ichazo and his school of enlightenment, Arica. I was very interested to hear about this when she came home. Typical of late-stage alcoholics, I had vague spiritual yearnings. It is no accident that alcohol is also called "spirits." Alcoholism and other addictions are a disease of the spirit, a broken spirit in which head and heart are separated by a vast ocean of pain, a disease in which behavior is no longer authentic.

I went to the 40-day Arica training after selling my boat-building business. I learned to relax, breathe, and meditate. I became a zealous seeker of higher states of consciousness and self-awareness. I felt reborn. I cut my hair and shaved off my beard. I learned two supportive ideas that have stayed with me. One was that the evolution of humanity occurs by attraction to higher levels of functioning. It does not happen gradually but in sudden "jumps" from one level to the next. Another idea was that I was participating in that evolution as a seeker. I continued seeking for 15 years, through different levels of the school, until I left Arica to go into treatment.

However, being a seeker is not a bed of roses. I was shocked to discover how much of a perfectionist and arrogant controller I was on the outside, and how much I hated myself on the inside. I saw my own silent screaming. It was very, very difficult for me to admit to anyone that I was in trouble with myself or that I might be vulnerable.

I also ignored the fact that this school had attracted the drug subculture. The marketing phrase the school used at that time was "get high

My self-image during the Arica 40-day

without drugs." I am guessing that people like myself who were feeling troubled by their use of drugs came to the school, bringing their drugs and alcohol with them. Strangely enough, mood-altering chemicals were not prohibited. I saw pot, alcohol, cocaine, and psychedelics circulating freely among the students. Then stories circulated about Ichazo's penchant for liquor and his hospitalization for liver problems. I began to suspect he could be an alcoholic. I questioned the validity of all that I had learned.

I had the delusion that I was better than people outside this cult, this new family to which I belonged, and that my mission was to spread the "We are One" message to the non-believers. It was quite literally spiritual abuse that I then heaped upon Barbara, who became convinced she also had to do the trainings and join the school in order to stay with me.

In spite of what I was learning, I continually fought with ongoing depression, disillusionment, and repressed anger. If I were so smart, enlightened, and sensitive, why was my life such a mess? I was irresponsible toward my family, and our relationships were shutting down.

In desperation to save my marriage and rescue myself from such unhappiness, I participated in a smorgasbord of self-development workshops. I went through Werner Erhard's *"est"* training in which I learned my definition of hell is isolation. That was followed by a prosperity training, a sexuality training,

affirmations, and the hot water rebirthing experience that took me back into the memory of my decision to not trust anyone shortly after I was born. Not one of these trainings suggested that I give up alcohol or drugs, nor did they have any real effect on my life other than to increase my disillusionment with myself.

After a separation and a failed attempt at reconciliation, our marriage ended in 1978. Chris was 7 years old when I told him of our first separation. I believe the shock to his psyche threw him off balance physically. He hurt himself badly by falling off a stool in the kitchen while talking on the phone to a friend. His forehead hit the edge of a counter, and we took him to the emergency room for stitches. As our marriage approached its final ending, I foolishly exposed Chris to wind and rain, hitch-hiking with him while he was sick. This resulted in his first major hospitalization. He developed a high fever and a strange swelling in the side of his throat that the doctors could not diagnose.

Barbara told me recently that I never physically hurt her, but that I had frightened her and sometimes terrified her with my anger, which mimicked the behavior of her alcoholic father. She came to believe that I hated her. My blaming and belittling wore down her self-esteem. I told her she was the one who was insane, not me, and in many ways she would "never be good enough." I had complained about her cooking and at the same time forced her to improvise low-cost meals because my attitude towards employment kept us in poverty. I had threatened her life with car accidents and careless driving, and yet I expected her to ride with me around Portland on a borrowed motorcycle late at night while I was high on LSD. She recalled many times when I demonstrated no empathy for her feelings, such as the time I refused to defend her against someone who was yelling irrational accusations at her, or the time I ignored her sadness for a vase that had been broken by some "nutso" people who had been invited into our home by me. She felt betrayed by my lack of interest in her and how the adventurous person that I had been at first became a grim, disdainful, demanding, careless and ungrateful husband. At the end of our marriage, she had begun to see me, correctly, as an overgrown child in her care. In addition, I could not be trusted to provide safety and well-being for our own son. It was time to leave.

We divided property and child custody with very little argument, and the judge rubber-stamped our decree. I was the only one in the courtroom at the end. I was feeling bitter, betrayed, helpless, and friendless. I could not see what I had done to my family, nor what I had done to myself.

I pursued other women, created arguments, started jobs that ended quickly because I couldn't tolerate working with others. I tried to start a restaurant business and failed. I began secretive smoking of marijuana on a bong. I suspected that I had become seriously addicted, but the shame of that thought prevented me from ever thinking about treatment or asking for help.

I abandoned my responsibility as a father and failed to keep the shared custody arrangements, so for many years of his young life, Chris relied on other male role models.

I started to run again, driving up and down the West coast on the Interstate while intoxicated, looking for love, looking for home, looking for God knows what. I think God may have seriously tried to get my attention one day. I was high on marijuana, and literally high above the Willamette River on a bridge in Portland when I didn't notice that the truck which I was passing on the right was about to change lanes. I was in a small Datsun, so when the truck hit my left rear corner, I was pushed into a spin across the front of the truck and smacked a second time.

The truck kept on going. Did the driver not even see me because he was loaded on pot like me, or was it because my car was so small and his viewpoint was so high above the road? The policeman who took my report didn't seem to notice I was stoned. Even though the car was beat up and missing the glass out of the rear window it was still drivable, and all I got was a stiff neck. Perhaps God was there, shielding me from death one more time.

With the insurance money from the car I went on to Los Angeles. I found a place where I could curl up in bed and feel myself drowning in self-pity for days on end. If someone came knocking on my door to attempt to rescue me, I would fly into a rage, and yet when I witnessed a young man like myself attempt suicide, I reassured myself that I wasn't as crazy as he was. At the same time, I was acutely aware of my mental confusion and the uselessness of drugs for solving my problems. I had a decent job, and yet I foolishly and arrogantly quit, accusing the owner of not knowing what they were doing. Then one day I crashed my bike into a car because I was riding too fast, out of control. I ran again. I did a "geographic escape" back to Eugene.

At the age of 37, I was living alone in a tiny, run-down, two-room shack. I was smoking at least 20 bong hits per day, and drinking at least 4 beers a day. I tried to be self-employed as a sign-maker, which amounted to self-unemployment most of the time. I would engage in heated arguments with my customers. One of my customers, Valerie, asked me to build a wood shower in her house. She would cook dinner for me at the end of the day, and I would leave soon after we finished eating. I was afraid of developing any intimacy even though I was attracted to her. After a period of getting acquainted and more deeply involved, I moved in with her. I was immediately gripped with fear, and moved out again in less than 24 hours.

The conflicts within me became reflected externally in a tumultous relationship with Valerie. We argued and fought constantly, followed by kissing and making up. We argued about money because I had become dependent upon her for financial support. We fought about jealousy because my attention would wander to other women. My verbal abuse escalated to physical abuse. I pushed her up against a wall, and threatened her with a hot iron.

My self-pity was the center of my life, and I would wallow in it, crying by myself, becoming apathetic, eating poorly, getting confused and physically run down. I began to worry about dying, either accidentally or deliberately from violence against myself. My coordination wasn't so good, and once I cut the tip off my finger while slicing potatoes. Sometimes as I was waiting to fall asleep I would feel my heart skip beats or stop for a moment. I had hemorrhoids, chronic snot in my nose, sore muscles, bursitis, and a sour stomach in the mornings. I mentioned the 20-plus bong hits per day to my doctor, and he shrugged it off, saying, "Whatever gets you through the night." I was shocked that he didn't recognize my covert plea for help. Perhaps he also smoked pot, I thought.

Several times I would try to quit, and I would get to about 10 days clean and then be consumed with an intolerable rage, mostly directed at myself, that would drive me back to smoking for relief. I couldn't get high from it any more, I would just feel numb. The same thing was happening with alcohol. I would mix 4 or 5 stiff drinks of vodka and frozen, concentrated limeade with no water, and I would feel lively for a short time, but I couldn't seem to get drunk. When Valerie suggested that I needed intensive, inpatient treatment, I flew into a rage and slapped her in the face. She ran out of the house. I had never slapped anyone in the face before, and I was shocked again. What was happening to me?

Legal problems began to appear in my life. I had been ticketed for an open container in the car, and I had also failed to appear on a previous citation for not wearing a lifejacket in a boat. Then I made an illegal left turn right in front of a cop while I was stoned and in the midst of an argument with Valerie. I made some evasive, sarcastic remarks to the policeman after he stopped me. He looked up my record on the computer in his patrol car. Then he ordered me to submit to a frisking and surprised me with tight, painful handcuffs. Next, he took me downtown for a booking. I was crying in the back seat. This had never happened to me before. Fortunately, I was not charged with driving under the influence of intoxicants. The only charge was the illegal turn. For the first time, I was in jail and frightened, but Valerie posted my bail. I was near my bottom, a higher bottom than some addicts who go to prison for felony crimes or hospitals from near-death vehicular crashes, and yet every bottom is equally painful and terrifying.

My son Chris, now 16 years old, asked me why he should respect me, and why did I smoke and drink? To answer him, I began to write while intoxicated, and the arrogant, defensive rubbish that I was putting down did nothing more than illuminate how lonely and hurt I felt. It was staring me in the face. Coupled with this awareness was the guilt and shame I felt for never being the kind of father I thought he should have and which I seemed powerless to provide. I had never kept the joint custody agreement with his mother, and I only saw him sporadically at long intervals. He had every right to not respect me.

The suicidal thoughts that I had at Dartmouth in 1961, the thoughts from which I sought relief through mood-altering drugs and alcohol, could no longer be held down. The alcohol and the marijuana didn't work any more. I became suicidal again. I was in hell, and I am here to tell you hell is just part of a much longer journey.

Shortly before I entered treatment, my sister arrived for a visit. Rebecca began to share with me how, as a Presbyterian minister, she had been in training to be a counselor and chaplain at a treatment center and had become familiar with the 12 steps of Alcoholic Anonymous. This had affected her unfinished grief process surrounding our father's death. As we talked about Daddy, we began to cry together, and I finally had enough trust to confess to someone I cared about that I had a problem with drugs and alcohol. She encouraged me to continue seeking help. I went to two treatment intake assessments and my first 12-step meeting. I could sense a big change about to happen in my life, and I was scared.

I had never been to a Catholic church service, but I was feeling this tremendous need to unload my burden of guilt, so I went and asked for confession, which was granted. The priest listened intently and kept asking me to slow down, slow down, as I blurted out my sins in a fount of tears.

At the same time, Chris developed a swelling in the side of his throat, the same swelling that had hospitalized him 8 years previously when I had separated from his mother. Was Chris manifesting in his body the frustration and anger about the loss of his family? Was the anger literally stuck in his throat? In retrospect, this became the "perfect storm" to drive me into treatment. God was trying to get my attention, again. He doesn't give up easily.

I found out I was accepted for treatment. I wanted to go in immediately, but felt that I had to remain with Chris until his medical crisis was over. I had been losing sleep for four or five nights. Finally, we took him to the hospital for exploratory surgery. I was anxiously waiting at the hospital, wrung out with adrenalin, fear, worry and guilt. Then the doctor told me they had found nothing and were concerned that the swelling was closing his airway. They needed my permission to do a tracheotomy. I signed the papers and then fell apart. I visited Chris in post-op. He had tubes in his arm and in his nose, wires hooked to machines, and I feared the worst, that he would die. The hospital bill of $7,000 was not covered by insurance, and they couldn't diagnosis the cause of the swelling. I talked to the hospital chaplain, who told me to take care of myself and surrender my son's medical problems to the doctors and God. That's when I gave the car keys to Valerie. My world was crashing, and I couldn't think straight. I wanted to die, I wanted to live.

I went to bed that midnight and slept for only an hour and a half. I woke with the certainty that I could delay treatment no longer, and began to pack a backpack. I was going to walk the 20 blocks to the treatment center. I left notes for Valerie. I didn't want to wake her to say goodbye because I was so full of shame. As I walked through Amazon Park in the early morning hours, I cried and roared, hysterical with grief for the impending loss of my lifestyle, my drug-using friends, possibly my wife and everything that was familiar. I felt very crazy. To me it felt like jumping off a cliff with no knowledge of how I would survive the landing nor where it would be.

I had been actively using alcohol and other drugs for 24 years, but the disease of chemical dependency began long before I ever picked up my first drink and will continue to haunt me for the rest of my life. The violence that I experienced in my childhood became internalized as violence against myself. I would work hard and then sabotage any chance of success. I suppressed my self-pity behind a mask of silence and lies. In my attempt to control my intolerable negative thoughts and feelings with drugs, I lost control of my behavior. The violence spilled out onto the people around me as denial, arrogance, irritation, criticism, sarcasm, anger, and temper tantrums that sometimes became physical. If I was offended by anyone, I would plot my revenge. I thought love was rescuing people inferior to myself. I chose relationships with people who could be easily victimized or who could provoke my self-image as victim. I was a mess, a very sick person, tied up in knots, never peaceful, always fighting, always lonely and sad, expecting failure. Worst of all, I would never reveal my inner torment to anyone.

Fortunately, I had access to treatment and the 12-step program which has given hope to millions of people like myself. What the world needs now is a treatment program for 7 billion people that would interrupt the dependency on domination and violence, provide the opportunity to heal the damages, and place the behavioral disease into remission. Can this be done? I repeat my challenge to you: if I can recover from violence, you can do it also, and if we can do it together, our entire culture can do this.

Our culture of violence

If you live in the United States and you think you have never been in hell, or that hell is where you go after you die, I suggest that you reconsider. We Americans have a reputation around the globe as one of the most violent of nations. We have a cultural disease, an epidemic of violence carried by the virus of disrespect. When we make mistakes, do we blame and attack others instead of seeing the opportunity to learn? I think so. I believe we are plagued with fears about not being good enough, not doing it right and not having the right answers. In attempting to divert attention from our embarrassment, we only make it worse. We

become helpless, angry victims. This leads to violence that is interpersonal, systemic and international.

Violence needs to be identified as a weakness in our national character. We need a prevention strategy for violence at all levels, from our homes and schools to our prisons, police and military, similar to the way we use prevention to protect our personal health. We could redirect *trillions* of dollars from death and destruction into growth and development.

The Global Peace Index for 2011 has the most recent and comprehensive summary of the degree to which the United States and 152 other nations are suffering from violence.[18] Using 23 qualitative and quantitative indicators, the index shows an increase in world violence for the third straight year and has placed the U.S. at number 82, far behind its European allies. The measurement of violence is not limited to international conflicts and military expenditure. It also includes internal, domestic conflicts, violent crime, prevalence of weapons, rates of incarceration and degrees of public safety.

The most common measures of the degree of violence have been the monetary costs of responding to it, or the savings that might have been realized in the absence of violence. Had the world been at peace in 2011, there would have been more than $8 trillion available to address some of our most pressing social problems. Simply reducing violence by 25 percent could produce an annual peace dividend of $2 trillion.

The Illinois Center for Violence Prevention estimated in 1993 that the direct and indirect costs of interpersonal violence in America was $425 billion[19] annually. This includes the costs of police, courts, prisons, private security systems, lost jobs, urban decay,

[18] Global Peace Index, Institute for Economics and Peace, 2011.

[19] http://www.icvp.org/fs_cost.asp

property loss, medical care, lost productivity, lost quality of life and mental health care. In 2009, the "average cost per murder exceeded $17.25 million and the average murderer...posed costs approaching $24 million. The most violent and prolific offenders *singly* produced costs greater than $150–160 million in terms of victim costs, criminal justice costs, lost offender productivity, and public willingness-to-pay costs."[20]

A 2004 World Heath Organization report estimates the cost to the U.S. government of interpersonal violence in the U.S. at more than $300 billion per year. The cost to victims was estimated at more than $500 billion per year. Combined, this is the equivalent to nearly 10% of the country's Gross Domestic Product (GDP).[21]

The United States is heavily invested in military domination of the world that is even more expensive. For Fiscal Year 2012, the White House has requested $558 billion for the Department of Defense, plus $118 billion for Iraq and Afghanistan. When the costs are included for nuclear weapons, counter-terrorism activity, homeland security, intelligence gathering, veterans' needs and pensions, military foreign aid, and the costs of borrowing to pay for all that, the known national security budget of the United States is just over *$1.2 trillion!*[22]

The past and future budgetary costs of the Mid-Eastern wars has been estimated at nearly $4 trillion by Brown University's Watson Institute for International Studies.[23] The full, indirect costs in lost lives, productivity and damage to infrastructure, property and the environment has never been calculated.

If you wish to see some more current statistics, read a 16-page report available online, *"Violence as a Public Health Risk."*[24] These numbers are hard to comprehend and yet may help us look at our own denial about the level of violence to which we have become numb. Does hell seem so far away and distant now?

My personal perception is that in the last 60 years America has slid into the bottom, the hell, of the addiction to violence dependency. Most of us are helplessly entangled in one form of violence or another as witness, victim or perpetrator. The violence has become systemic, embedded in our media, laws and policies. We have become complicit with it. It could be termed "domination disorder" in order to be more inclusive of the verbal, psychological, mental, emotional, spiritual, and systemic forms of violence.[25]

The dependency on domination behavior is structurally no different than an individual's addiction to chemicals, sex, work, or danger.[26] However, the vast scale of it, the epidemic

---

[20] DeLisi, M. et al, Murder by numbers: monetary costs imposed by a sample of homicide offenders, The Journal of Forensic Psychiatry & Psychology Vol. 21, No. 4, August 2010, 501–513

[21] The Economic Dimensions of Interpersonal Violence, World Health Organization, 2004

[22] Hellman, C., $1.2 Trillion for National Security, http://www.tomdispatch.com, March 1, 2011,

[23] http://costsofwar.org/

[24] Haegerich and Dahlberg, Violence as a Public Health Risk, American Journal of Lifestyle Medicine, 2011 5:392 available at http://ajl.sagepub.com/content/5/5/392

[25] Schaef, A. W., When Society Becomes an Addict, HarperOne, 1988

[26] Cf. Velez-Mitchell & Mohr, Addict Nation, Health Communications Inc., Deerfield Beach, FL, 2011 and Gilligan, J., Violence, Vintage, 1997

nature of the addiction, brings with it culturally-supported denial. We hear rationalizations that tell us that violence is not a problem, that it is normal, inevitable, or necessary. We are told that *we* are not violent, *other* people are violent. Some people equate peace with weakness. War is the accepted norm and is glorified. Nightmares about nuclear weapons are trivialized in exchange for a false sense of strength and security. "Freedom isn't free" appears on bumper stickers and T-shirts, oblivious to the social and economic prison we have created for ourselves. There is a cynicism about applying the values of our founding fathers -- equality, justice and the common defense -- to ALL people on the planet. Applying the Golden Rule is considered optional.

The truth is that, as a nation and as a planet, we live in addictive, repeating cycles of violence and war, repeating the same mistakes and expecting different results, living out the insanity and self-destructive culture of violence. If we are to survive as a nation, and some would say survive as a species, we must return to health. Species of life may be going extinct at a projected rate of anywhere from 83 to over 300 per day, depending on how the data is gathered.[27] Who is to say that mankind, with enough nuclear bombs to destroy all life on the planet several times over, shall not be one of them? We are trapped in a spiral of self-dependence and lack of trust. Real progress will never be made until we reduce our level of fear. Violence is a useless strategy for resolving conflict. Violence is not power. Violence is a weakness. It is a tool of cowards and bullies. It does not create control, it releases chaos. The culture of violence needs to be replaced, not overwhelmed with police powers, not corrected with underfunded agencies, not locked up in a

jail cell, not treated as somebody else's problem. It's our problem.

Some activists are joining the global movements to alter this culture. The movements for peace, civil rights, women's equality, and care for the environment are all efforts to recover. However, even the pacifist who is willing to die to avoid harming another may be unwittingly violent in the pursuit of that agenda.

I have been continually reminded, by working for peace, of my own desire to dominate. Coming from the desire to be right, I have used opinionated thoughts, words and deeds, denial and bluffing. I have sometimes felt that I was uniquely different or better than others who did not match my idea of peace-monger. Because I did not accept others as equals, I became isolated behind the walls of judgment and opinion. I have undermined my own progress towards peace because my fears of confrontation kept me from realizing the potential for collaboration. I have been, and still am, a recovering violent person.

The culture of violence is passed down through the generations within families. For example, in my childhood there was a double standard for violence. Daddy was a rage-aholic who could explode with verbal or physical abuse and terrify the kids. For myself, my brother and sister, having a temper tantrum was not allowed.

I adopted the posture of a victim. Then I projected my victim identity onto everyone around me. I learned to be just like Daddy, in spite of my best efforts not to do so. I became part of the culture. I became intimidating, controlling, manipulative and even violent to get my needs met. Empathy and compassion were not in my behavioral vocabulary. I had few friends, felt like an outcast and was filled with anger towards everyone, including myself. I was filled with toxic shame. I became suicidal and turned to drugs and alcohol to numb the pain,

---

[27] http://www.whole-systems.org/extinctions.html

which is simply suicide on the installment plan and another form of violence against oneself. Of course, I periodically vented that culture of violence upon anyone else within range.

There has not been, and still is not, a significant mainstream culture to intervene on family violence and to support non-violence within families. The public and private agencies working on the issue are pushing upstream against a strong current. We grow up in a culture of violence and pass it from generation to generation. In our nation and in our world, violence is spiraling out of control. Where does it end? Now there is little money for prevention, programs that should have been funded years ago, programs that would have paid for themselves many times over in reduced cost to the community and the criminal justice system. Restorative justice reduces or prevents recidivism. Alcohol and drug treatment often prevents violent or property crime. Conflict resolution education in schools can reduce or prevent bullying. Parenting education is correlated with fewer numbers of delinquent children. Relationship counseling and anger management helps to prevent domestic violence and high rates of divorce.

Most of us view the violence in our society as normal. We need to question our assumptions about the differences between normal and healthy behavior, and open our vision to a legacy of peace for our children. Only when something truly stunning happens, like the attack on the World Trade Center towers on 9/11, a school shooting with multiple victims, or the attempt to publicly assassinate Arizona Representative Giffords, do we grope for words adequate to the situation. Only then do we begin to feel our feelings, identify our feelings, and start to act on our feelings instead of our old opinions and judgments. Unfortunately for many Americans, the previous notions about violence, perpetrators, and victims return quickly and we may need to be stunned many times before we

begin to look in earnest for the underlying causes. On the other hand, many people are now waking up to honest, authentic heart communication as worthy of a sustained effort. This new awareness is my hope for survival in the face of our imminent self-destruction if we do not change our violent trajectory.

We need to realize that cooperation and mutual respect are better strategies for security and survival than competition and mutual destruction. We live in a time of great crisis and great fear. We commonly lack the skills to make a friend from an enemy, so enemies multiply endlessly, and we cower or we explode. The greatest war, the greatest terror and enemy that we have to face is within ourselves, from the President to the members of Congress, to the tormented student and the abused child. There is a very dark and deep abyss within the soul of America. The illness, the cancer, of violent habits of thoughts, words and actions which are tearing our communities apart every day is destroying our trust in human values and decency, and building a metaphoric time bomb of cataclysmic proportions.

Let us take the crucial first step, let us move forward to end this insanity, let's admit we have a problem. Then we can move ahead, one step at a time.

Step 2: Trust the process

2. Believe that a power greater than yourself can bring you strength and peace.

My first challenge upon entering treatment was to simply accept the care of people who knew more than I did about my disease, and to have just a bit of faith that recovery was possible. Now that I had taken the giant first step in admitting I had a problem, was I going to believe there was a solution?

I was shocked by what had happened and the events that quickly unfolded. I thought I was tough, but I couldn't even stand up at the nurses' station in the treatment center as the fear of what I was doing hit me in the knees. I had been drawing what I thought was a doodle on a pad of paper, when suddenly the line became the story of my life, spiraling away from my center and off into oblivion. I was suddenly very afraid.

I thought I had a minor problem. I

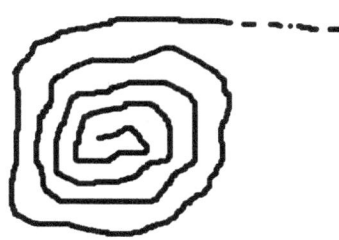

thought I had already detoxed in the few days since my last drink. In reality, I had probably stalled my detox symptoms with the adrenalin from worry about Chris and his medical emergency. The treatment center had a small hospital ward for a medically-supervised detoxification process. There was a nurse's station and nearby beds. Everyone entering treatment was required to stay there until cleared by the doctor. I thought I didn't need it, and yet for two days I was in an angry delirium, going through repeating, out-of-control cycles of anger

with sweating, followed by chills with crying and shaking. I threatened the nurses with running out the door to die if they didn't pay more attention to me. I had nightmares. I told a counselor that I felt like I was in the seventeenth level of hell. The counselor told me to try prayer.

Not since I had asked God to prove his existence to me by blinding me had I prayed. I had nothing to lose. I asked God to help me break the cycle of anger, sweats, shaking and chills. It worked! I started to calm down almost immediately. I had taken my first baby step toward a faith in a higher power.

When I finally went downstairs to eat in the cafeteria with the other patients, I shuffled around hugging a pillow as if it were my teddy bear, and I avoided eye contact with anyone. On my third day there, they gave me back my clothes. I started to gain some confidence that I had made the right choice by entering treatment. As I received education about the nature of addiction, the fog of confusion began to clear, although I still felt something was basically wrong with my personality. I didn't understand that what I had was a disease. I began to eat properly, and get some daily exercise. During Family Week I began to heal my relationships with Valerie, Chris, and my mother.

Because the schedule was packed with lectures, small groups, homework and very little time alone, four weeks of treatment passed quickly. When it was time to leave, I was extremely grateful to the staff and the other patients with whom I had bonded. We were the lucky ones, the survivors. Many, many addicts are never identified or get treatment. They end up in jails, mental institutions or death.

Life was fragile during the first weeks and months after treatment. For Valerie and I, our greatest fear was that we would return to our homeostatic patterns in our relationship. We became hyper-vigilant to any signs of co-dependency, enabling or argument. Valerie was terrified that I might hit her again. She and I attended once-a-week aftercare counseling for the first 12 months as the best support for getting solidly into recovery, and we looked forward to those meetings. We learned how to take the focus off of each other and put it onto ourselves, so that we could make "I feel" statements instead of "you always" accusations. The arguments still continued, and yet with the help of the aftercare group process the intensity never reached the extreme peaks of anger we had known before treatment.

I found a home meeting in a 12-step recovery group that was a step study. I struggled with my self-consciousness and lingering guilt, so I didn't talk much. I remained hidden behind my mask. I mostly listened, and kept going, out of a feeling of duty to Valerie and my counselor. I wasn't attending because I enjoyed recovery. It was work. I got a sponsor who was perfect for me because he made me work the steps. Every time I saw him he would make me accountable to my progress. He was my polar opposite, a leather-jacketed biker with missing teeth. I respected him, but eventually he started moving around so that I couldn't always reach him, and I found another sponsor.

I knew self-employment was a high-risk situation for me because of the isolation, the unpredictable income, and the difficulties I had with promoting myself, so I went to a community college class in career exploration. The class seemed to raise more questions than provide answers for me, so I didn't finish the class and began a job search instead. I had experience in sign-making and wood-working, so I looked in those areas without success. Then one day I saw an opening for a darkroom assistant, and although I doubted my abilities, I was given the opportunity. I gratefully accepted this small miracle. It turned out to be a perfect fit because I was mostly working alone as a technician doing something I enjoyed, in the dark, listening to the radio. I only needed to interact with co-workers or my boss at long intervals, so I could develop working relationships gradually. One co-worker was easy to relate to, because she shared with me that she was the adult child of an alcoholic, and we had great conversations.

It felt incredibly good to have a stable routine at last, with a steady income. I began to repay my debts for Chris' hospital bills, pay my share of current living expenses, and have a little pocket money for myself. My sponsor helped me to use the recovery steps for working through a crisis with my boss. I was able to see my part in it, and detach from his part in it. I didn't feel compelled to quit, as I would have done in my using days. My self-esteem was rising. Valerie and I were beginning to have fun and enjoy each other more.

However, I wasn't completely free of the THC, the active ingredient in marijuana which had lodged in the fat cells of my body. As the blood and the liver slowly eliminated it, there was never enough to even hint at feeling high, but I would feel a tight, numb sensation in my head and a lethargy in my body. These feelings would continue to come and go for about a year and a half after treatment. I still dreamt about pot and using friends. I would wake up feeling guilty and reminded of how recovery is difficult and slow work. I was very pleased one day when I woke from a dream in which I refused both drugs and money in favor of authentic love. Fortunately, I had no urges to use when I was awake, and I would actually feel slightly nauseous if I smelled someone's second-hand pot smoke, or the alcohol vapors from their drink in a restaurant.

In my third month clean and sober, I started seeing a private therapist in addition to my 12-step recovery group meetings and aftercare. I felt like I was turning a new leaf, away from guilt and toward forgiveness and a positive outlook. I slowly learned to talk about my feelings. I chaired a few 12-step meetings and began to feel more comfortable in large groups of strangers. At six months clean, my relationship with Chris made some significant progress toward healing, and at eight months Valerie was ready to have a baby. I was amazed that her trust level had gone up that much. I was still uncertain about my ability to be an adequate father.

I also discovered that I had replaced drugs and alcohol with food, especially sweets and carbohydrates, my new comforters. I had gained 25 pounds during my first year. I didn't celebrate my one-year-clean date. I was afraid of not getting attention, and I was afraid of getting it. I was afraid of success, afraid that if I received acknowledgement, my own deep belief in my incompetence would rise up to sabotage it. Yet everybody in my last aftercare group said loving things about me: *"perceptive, warm, wise, caring, strong, unlimited potential, hardest worker ever in the program."*

In spite of my lack of trust in myself and the recovery process, I had begun to separate myself from my disease. This process of separation has been gradual and sometimes excruciatingly slow. Seven years after treatment, I had a dream that helped to externalize my fear of failure, like puss oozing from a wound as part of its healing. In my dream, I was at a 12-step meeting in which I sensed hypocrisy. Somebody couldn't recite the 6th Step, and all the men were dressed alike. I heard someone explain how a drink or two wasn't harmful. I went to a bar, and became very intoxicated. I felt guilty, alarmed, and scared. I went looking for someone to whom I could confess this relapse into drinking, and when I found a fellow alcoholic, I could not talk, I could only make guttural noises. Another recovering person came up behind me and said, "You can never do what you want to do." I began to tantrum, hitting the floor with my fists. I woke up from the dream.

The dream told me I was scared of my own hypocrisy, scared of conformity, and scared of joining groups. I was scared of my own power of rationalization, scared of total surrender to a higher power and scared of my own impotence. As I wrote these thoughts down on paper, they began to lose their power.

By working the second step, I became ready to accept that I didn't have all the answers, and that something or somebody outside myself did. My fears of being punished or humiliated for being wrong began to relax. I became open to the possibility that I could have a higher power that was gently life-giving and life-promoting, that forgave my mistakes, and that I could trust for support. All of my previous life experiences from my childhood onwards had conditioned me to never trust, and here I was, getting ready to trust an unknown and unknowable something, a process I did not understand. Part of me was asking, was I being set up for a big fall? Of course, I was terrified by Step Two!

All of the stories I had been told about Santa Claus and the Easter Bunny had turned out to be empty fabrications with no impact on how we really lived our lives. I had abandoned organized religion for over 30 years because of the hypocrisy I saw. I had become successful at manipulating and controlling other people with my anger tantrums, my seductive people-pleasing, and my analytical rationalizations. Why would I give that up now?

Well, the people around me in recovery seemed to have some serenity, some happiness and some relationship skills that I didn't have. Their struggles were smaller in size. They shared miracles of success with health, jobs, children, spouses and parents. These people were able to laugh at themselves! I couldn't do that. Like a moth drawn to the flame, I was being drawn forward to the dissolution of my distrust.

Step 3: Give up the struggle

3. Make a commitment to connect with a higher power, as you understand it, whether this higher power be understood as [the collective wisdom of a group], God, Yahweh, Allah, Buddha, Krishna, Mother Earth-Father Sky, The Divine, or whatever understanding brings you strength and peace.

> *My own hands imprison me....*
> *Yeah I'm here without a name*
> *In the palace of my shame*
> *I said love rescue me*
> — Bono & Bob Dylan

When we refuse to recognize and accept the love and support of a power greater than ourselves, when we fiercely defend our self-centered independence, we become like defiant children. Letting go of the struggle against external enemies and our status as a victim is not easy because it locates the primary enemy within ourselves, the last place we would want to find it. As Walt Kelly's cartoon character, Pogo, said, *"We have found the enemy, and he is us."*

It took two years of going to 12-step meetings for me to take my first tentative step toward giving up my defiance. Between jobs I had spent a few months as a hospice volunteer and my role was to regularly visit two men that were dying of cancer. They had polar opposite viewpoints on their impending death. One of them had the attitude of one day at a time and died peacefully. The other was angry and resentful. He died thrashing against the restraints placed upon him by hospital staff. Witnessing this difference caused me to examine how I wanted to be as I approached my own death.

The point labeled "surrender," where the upward line of emotional balance surges into positive territory (p. 42), occurred for me one day when I realized that my secret plan to get loaded at the age of 92 and go out in a fog of chemicals wasn't such a good idea. Perhaps I wanted something better than that. This secret was holding me hostage from further growth in recovery, and I had to let it go. Later on, when I saw similarity between the Campbell graph of grief (p. 25) and the one I had drawn of my addiction and recovery process, I could see the moment that I surrendered my secret as the point at which I let go and crossed over into increasingly positive emotional states.

I shared this secret with my sponsor and then shared it more publicly, with my home group. I finally surrendered to the fact that I would be in recovery for the rest of my life and I would never return to using mood-altering chemicals. Recovery began to be rewarding as I finally got the courage to share more in meetings. I realized that by remaining silent I was only hurting myself, and that I was beginning to feel safe and secure as soon as I sat in my chair. I felt a sense of belonging, as if I were truly meant to be in that chair. It was no accident. I began to *own* my recovery, for me. I had been going to meetings to satisfy the expectations of my family and counselor. Now it was for me, not anyone else. I began to trust the collective wisdom of the group as a power greater than myself.

At the same time, I began to trust my future, which was beginning to look brighter and full of possibilities. I began a savings account without making any withdrawals right away, for the first time in my life. I opened a retirement account. I kept my job in the photo darkroom for two years, a record for me, and when it ended it wasn't because I quit or was fired. I was simply laid off due to lack of work. I was even given a good letter of recommendation. At first, the unstructured time of unemployment felt like a threat, but meetings, writing the steps and talking with my sponsor proved their value to me.

However, I still clung to the belief that I was in charge of my recovery. If anyone or anything was responsible for changing my life, it would be me. I slowly discovered how false was that idea. I wanted to begin the process of understanding my relationship to my higher power, whom I have always named as God because of my exposure to Christianity. For most of my life I had avoided this relationship out of fear, because I had identified God as a father figure. I believed that I had not even begun to earn the right to have any relationship with God. Obviously, I was not going to be comfortable around an all-powerful, all-knowing male because that was too close to a description of the person who had most abused me, Daddy.

The 12-step program taught me to alter my image of God into one that was more loving and supportive. My first experiment showed me how much I refused to accept that support. I decided to set the alarm on my digital watch to beep on the hour, every 60 minutes, as a reminder to myself. When I heard the beep I would say to myself, "Thy will, not mine, be done." Within a very short time I was appalled to discover how much I believed that my will was the key to making things happen. Within a few minutes after the reminder, I would attempt to take control of people and situations so events would proceed as I thought they should. I had zero humility! This awareness was the beginning of the end of my struggles.

Within a few years I had begun to visualize God as a gentle, friendly giant. Then I gave up anthropomorphic fantasies altogether, and for me God is now an indescribable combination of darkness, light, stillness and the energy of continuous creation. I want to allow God to define itself, reveal itself, without my arrogant belief that I could possibly understand God or ask God for favors.

When I get my impatient willfulness out of the way, God is full of surprises. I found employment that was far better than I expected, doing what I love to do, photography, with congenial and understanding co-workers. Friends and family whom I thought needed my help desperately were able to find their own way to health and wholeness without me. I began to sleep better, eat better, and get more done, effortlessly. I have received countless gifts of personal transformation in which character defects became their opposites. For example, timidity has become daring, silence has become assertiveness, cowardly manipulation has become ethical leadership, denial has become transparency, and self-doubt has become self-confidence.

Some time around my third year in recovery, I had a significant dream in which I had learned to not only constructively "see" with my heart, I could also see my Higher Power's will for me, see the work that needed to be done, and willingly bend to doing that hard work. This dream accurately forecast the direction my life would begin to take many years later. As I let go of my old, fierce self-reliance, I am able to feel a strength and peace that I never expected. Sometimes it now seems there is nothing else more important to do than to return to that peace.

I began attending church because Valerie had found a preacher that she liked and she wanted to share her experience with me. One Sunday, I was moved to tears by not only the pipe organ and the poetry of the hymns which evoked memories of singing in the choir of a grand cathedral in my childhood, but also the strong feeling that I had found a community of seekers like myself who were willing to entertain doubts and questions. This church, like the 12-step program, was non-dogmatic about the definition of God. Within a few years I surprised myself by becoming a member of that church, surprised because I had rejected organized religion as false when I was a teenager.

I also experimented with shamanic journeying for several months, and made a practice of recording my dreams. Always, I found that the intensity of my spiritual quest, the effort, would get in my way. I thought of myself as some kind of warrior-monk, out to win the battle for love and God. I would forget that I carried inside myself a major case of toxic shame, that I didn't need to try so hard to do it perfectly, that I could just relax into it. Quite honestly, I didn't know how to completely relax, and I kept looking for better relaxation methods.

My struggle to trick myself into giving up the struggle, as paradoxical as that may sound, still continues to this day. I am still learning to truly listen and be part of my community. Around fourteen years into recovery I began to feel "spiritually stagnant." I felt that I was no longer growing in recovery and I was also fearing relapse if I should ever stop going to 12-step meetings once a week. Fortunately, my treatment center asked me to share my recovery story with patients on a regular basis, which helped me to see how far I had traveled on the recovery path. It was during this time that I developed the graphical representation of my story to help me in the telling of it. I also tried to renew my meditation practice and was shocked to find how tyrannical, aggressive, and hyper-vigilant were the thoughts spinning in my head.

A wonderfully relaxing Watsu manipulation[28] in a warm-water pool helped to open my heart and eyes to realize that love and trust are the same. I became more determined than ever to follow my quest for deeper connection with my soul and the spirit world, and yet I would be periodically thrown into self-doubts, fears, and family conflicts. The issue of what constituted fair sharing of household expenses continued to wrench my relationship with Valerie. However, the fact that we were both attending 12-Step recovery meetings and talking to our sponsors has made all the difference and kept our marriage intact.

When Michael was in middle school and teaching me some hard lessons about parenting, I felt very incompetent sometimes and was terrified that he would repeat the mistakes that I had made. I became ill with a yeast overgrowth in my intestinal tract, went to an acupuncturist, and under his care withdrew from sugar and all sweet, fruity foods and juices for 30 days. I was shocked by the withdrawal symptoms I experienced, and the strong cravings I had developed for sugars. My addiction to chemicals was more general than I had thought it was. Sugar is a mood-altering substance!

My life has continued to get better through many ups and downs. My relationship with my two sons has healed to the point where they are seeking my advice and sending me loving Father's Day cards. My older son, Chris, has become a non-violent, kind and generous father in spite of his exposure to the verbal and physical violence of my parenting. I am very grateful that the cycle of violence in my family has broken and I've become my own better parent.

It may be that our first baby step toward trusting the process of recovery, trusting others, and trusting ourselves comes from a sense of desperation in a situation that seems to be dangerous, completely out of control and unmanageable. As that desperation grows, we may begin to wonder how real change takes place. How do we ever make any progress as individuals or as a society? What we are doing does not seem to be working, and may be making things worse. It is in these moments of lost hope, when we are most vulnerable, that new possibility creeps in.

---

[28] http://www.watsu.com

In most circumstances of desperation there is a strong temptation to simply give up. In our culture this is strongly condemned as a sign of weakness, yet it is precisely what needs to be done to regain the ground that has been lost, to repair the damage and assess our next strategy for moving forward to a life of nonviolence and peace. We must give up the struggle in order to win. We must finally, completely, and irrevocably say to ourselves, *"I don't know what to do next."* It is out of this not knowing that we discover new knowledge. Let me be clear that we never give up seeking better answers, we simply give up our hard-headed insistence that we already know the answers.

We arrive at true humility in this way when we surrender our certainty. Nobody has the right, true, ultimate answer to all our problems. This may seem at first to be a rather astounding realization. We are all in this trouble together and the solutions will come from all of us, nobody in particular.

Yet we fear being in community, in communion with others, where all our secrets, our shame and guilt, could be exposed. Unfortunately, tragically, by keeping a lid on our shame, we also keep a lid on our magnificence, our full potential as human beings.

> *"Our deepest fear is not that we are inadequate. Our deepest fear is that we are powerful beyond measure. It is our light, not our darkness that most frightens us. We ask ourselves, Who am I to be brilliant, gorgeous, talented, fabulous? Actually, who are you not to be?"*[29]

The work of achieving the freedom in which our best qualities shine forth is perhaps more difficult than possibly can be imagined because it has to do with letting go of our defiant desire to look, sound, and act in way that others would judge to be good, strong, or virtuous. When the only thing that truly matters is our relationship to our higher power, and when that relationship has become solid, so solid that trust is no longer an issue, we can let go of all our posturing, relax, and just be our natural selves.

Individual freedom comes from surrender to a process greater than anything we could devise on our own.

---

[29] Williamson, M., A Return to Love, Harper Paperbacks, 1996

Steps 4 - 6: Start with yourself

4. Make an honest moral inventory of how you have contributed to conflict and violence in your personal relationships, your life in community, and as a citizen of your country and the world. Accept the fact that often your best intentions result in unintended negative consequences upon other people.

5. Admit to your higher power, to yourself, and to others the exact nature of your contributions to conflict and to emotional or physical violence.

6. Focus more on the here and now. Slow down. Breathe deeply. Keep life and your conflicts in perspective. Become responsible for your feelings and behavior.

Steps Four through Six open the door to self-acceptance of ourselves just the way we are, without any judgement, in complete honesty. Step Four is about bringing into the light the inner demons, the unconscious, ineffective thoughts and behaviors that reinforce our addictive cycles. Naming them robs them of their power. Summoning the courage for Step Five, we humbly join the rest of humanity in the full experience of our broken lives. In Step Six we prepare to detach from perfectionism, blame, comparing ourselves to others and impossibly high standards of behavior. These steps do not result in immediate changes, although the difference in personality is remarkable when we look back at our progress over long periods of time. I primarily worked on the fourth, fifth, and sixth steps of the program in what I call the "middle years" of my recovery, starting around my third year. In the next 9 years I rewrote my responses to these inventory steps four or five times.

A moral inventory is simply the process of listing behaviors in two categories, negative and positive. It is very important to see ourselves as a mixture of light and dark. In my first inventory, I could not think of a single positive characteristic about myself. I looked at my gluttony, impatience, and arrogance. It wasn't until I wrote my second inventory that I realized it wasn't helpful for me to be carrying so much toxic shame and guilt, and it was time to practice letting go. Each time that I repeated the inventory process I was able to reveal a deeper layer of my recycling dysfunction. I learned that there are many things besides chemicals towards which I could exhibit addictive behavior, including food, work, sex, anger, and violence. When I had begun to step back from my own process far enough that I could see myself objectively, I drew my cycles of thoughts and feelings into the flow diagram of my addiction process (page 28).

At first I was very upset to re-visit these behaviors because they seemed so deeply imbedded within me. It didn't seem possible that I could ever get rid of them. For example, as a child I had decided to withhold my productive energy and creativity so that I would not be ridiculed or criticized for being less than wonderfully perfect in my accomplishments. When this issue came up as part of my inventory, it was difficult for me to accept that I had wasted years of my life hiding under a mask of incompetence, laziness, and rebellion. I felt strong feelings of grief for this self-inflicted loss. This had been an act of inner violence against myself. How could I avoid plunging into a well of self-pity? How could I risk replacing my childhood protection strategies with some really creative contributions? What if I failed?

However, the thought that I could not change myself was my old macho self-reliance and my toxic shame talking to me. This process of self-examination would turn out to be a shared process supported by my sponsor and my higher power. Working these steps meant not only doing a great deal of solitary self-examination, writing responses to questions, it also meant talking to my sponsor, prayer, and reading recovery books. I began to ask for and utilize outside help. I used an excellent workbook, *"The 12 Steps -- A Way Out,"*[30] in coordination with a small group of other recovering men and women who would meet weekly to reflect on what we had written. These resources provided me with the inspiration and courage that I needed. I still wanted to have all the right answers beforehand, and I went ahead anyway. As long as I still believed as I had been conditioned to believe -- that I was supposed to be happy and positive, repressing all my negative thoughts, feelings and behaviors -- I could not speak of my shame. I would be stuck.

"It's the awareness, the full experience . . . of how you are stuck, that makes you recover."
— Frederick S. Perls

I wrote in my workbook about my anxiety that came up in anticipation of working Step Four, and I went back to Step Three to make sure I was ready to have my higher power with me as I plunged onwards. I reviewed my forms of denial that kept me in the dark. I looked at my resentments and fears. Then I began to list both my strengths and my limitations as they related to my isolation, repressed anger, approval seeking, caretaking, controlling, fear of abandonment, fear of authority figures, frozen feelings, low self-esteem, overdeveloped sense of responsibility, and repressed sexuality. It was very comprehensive. I looked both at each problem in detail and at my vision for how I might specifically benefit from letting go of each one. This was work!

For example, I simply listed what I fear, what causes the fear and how that fear affects the way I think, feel and behave. I discovered that my fear of God affected my self-esteem because I might be judged as useless, worthless, stupid and impotent. These thoughts in turn activated deep shame, self-pity, envy of others and struggles for control. I had to let go of my fear of being punished. That was just one of many fears, and each one received the same close examination.

Getting a clear picture of how I not only expressed my anger but also repressed it gave me the ability to witness it as it happened. Clenched teeth, sarcasm, raising my voice, glaring, frowning, going silent -- all these symptoms became early warning signs that I was getting ready to explode with verbal or physical abuse. I became aware of how my anger contributed to my constant sadness and physical aches and pains. I saw how I attempted to control my father's unpredictable temper tantrums by attempting to please him constantly, and how my failure to do so became proof of my inadequacy. I realized that his death had made it impossible in my mind to ever win his approval, and that I could now work on accepting myself just the way I am. I became ready to be seen, accepted, and even loved by others for who I really am.

Within a relatively short time, I could talk about how I felt about a situation instead of what I thought about it. Instead of blaming others for my feelings, I could not only identify and own my feelings, I could explain specifically what I knew about myself. I knew why those feelings arose. I learned a whole new vocabulary from a list of words for feelings that was conveniently divided into words for positive and negative feelings, from weak to strong. I was no longer limited to sad, mad or glad.

---

30 Friends in Recovery, The 12 Steps - A Way Out, RPI Publishing, 1995.

As I increased my ability to accept my behaviors, I could even share them in groups, which is part of Step Five. I began to see the cyclical patterns in my behavior. The freedom I felt was exhilarating. I no longer had to have the safe, right answer to every situation or make up lies to compensate for not knowing. I could take the risk of guessing and, as I took more risks, I learned to listen to my intuition, the wisdom of others and my higher power, which improved the results of my guesswork.

It was at this time that I was laid off from the photo darkroom, and I took another risk, a customer service job at a one-hour photo lab. I learned to enjoy working under pressure and meeting the public. My fear of strangers was dissolving. I surprised myself with my ability to remember names and connect with people through small talk.

I began to form some rewarding friendships with other men in the program in early recovery. Someone asked me to be their sponsor, much to my surprise. I didn't think I had much to offer other than simple basics, and in truth that is all I really needed to know. I volunteered to answer the hotline where addicts in crisis could get the time and place for the next 12-step meeting and an empathetic ear, or at least my best attempt at empathy. It wasn't easy.

Then, I took the risk of applying for a counselor intern program at the treatment center where I had been a patient. This move propelled me into the center of intense social interaction where difficult issues of life and death were in my face. For someone who had chosen for most of his life to hide at the back of the room, I was amazed at how much I grew. Learning how to interview other people, learning how to listen, changed my life. Not only could I create some peace in the center of the maelstrom within myself, I could facilitate other people finding some of their own.

I wasn't sure I could be a better father than I had been, and yet attempting to have a child with Valerie was another risk I took. I had already given up on the notion of children when she surprised me with her desire to transform our couple into a family. She had previously told me that working with children all day as a classroom teacher was more than enough exposure to behavior problems. However, Valerie was changing her attitudes about herself as she progressed in her own 12-step recovery. Because she was 42, she had a greater risk of a failed pregnancy and her first one ended in a stillbirth. All the guilt and fears around our previous sexual misbehaviors and failings came rushing forth with the grief. We may have stopped there if it had not been for the support we were receiving from the 12-step program.

We tried again. Soon, my second son Michael was born into our joyful, grateful family and I began to re-learn how to be a father. We enrolled in a wonderful parenting education and support group, Birth To Three. Outside help was the only way we could learn new parenting skills to replace what our parents had shown us by example. The 12-step program had paved the way to accepting help.

Internalize new self-respect

Similarly, I needed to replace my negative beliefs about myself with encouraging ones, and I believed that I could not ask my friends or family for that kind of help. However, help sometimes comes in strange and mysterious ways, and it does come from outside myself. The most ironic thing happened as I was writing this paragraph. I received a phone call notifying me that I was to receive recognition as a Peacebuilder of the year at a local fundraiser event. This was the second such call in one month, and I was not only very surprised, I was frightened. It meant to me that people were actually watching and listening to me. I not only had some influence, I also had the responsibility to use it wisely. My self-confidence choked up for a short period of time, and then I accepted with awe and amazement the tremendous support and encouragement I was receiving.

When I realized after my first moral inventory that carrying excessive shame and guilt was toxic to my mental health, I began to use affirmations for several months to re-program my thoughts. I borrowed from several sources to compose my personal list of affirmations. I then tape-recorded myself speaking them out loud, and played them back often for several months until I felt I had substantially internalized what I was telling myself.

These are the affirmations that I used:

* I am a spiritual warrior: relaxed, alert, and peaceful.

* God loves me, and I trust God to care for me. I am lovable. I listen to the still, small, voice of God within me. I am consciousness.

* I listen to my aches and illness, my doubts and questions, my grief, guilt and anger, as urgings from my God for me to grow.

* My limits of power are the source of vitality in my relationship with God.

* I understand that everything continues to change, except for God, who is always there for me. I belong here.

* I am incomplete, and I am getting better and better every day in every way.

* I am always doing the best that I can with what I have in each moment, and I forgive myself for the mistakes that help me to learn and grow. I am capable. I am learning how to learn.

* I accept my successes and failures equally, as part of the adventure of life.

* I know that my experience of life as negative or positive is up to me, and I choose to make it positive. I take the time to notice and be grateful for the good things flowing my way.

* I keep a perspective when details become problematic. I am resilient, balanced.

* I know how and when to ask for help with my problems. My problems are my stepping stones to freedom.

* I have an invincible summer at the deepest part of winter in my life. I welcome my challenges.

* I am courageously facing my shame and fears of rejection. I choose a new way of life. I am willing to risk sharing my feelings and ideas.

* I accept and let go of my character defects so that I can nurture my needs. I am my own best friend, even to the parts of myself that I have rejected.

* I love and care for myself and my feelings.

* I am honest with myself about my anger, and find respectful ways to express it. I accept others' anger when it is directed at my behavior.

* I am patient, gentle, and compassionate with others and myself.

* I am walking out of isolation and into trusting, nurturing relationships. I am a warm and friendly person.

* I am grateful for, and take the time for, my relationships. I am not alone. I am surrounded by courageous people like myself. I praise them.

* I am vocal, vulnerable, and vital. I am persistent, strong, a survivor.

* It's great to be alive! I love to be physically active.

* I enjoy play, humor, fun and curiosity. I am involved in living. I love my wild and silly ideas.

* I am letting go of my desire for rational control.

*I have a creative initiative that follows my intuition. I am a productive, pioneering light unto the world. I am willing to share my holistic vision of life.

Detach from blame

It is very difficult for any of us to avoid the conditioning which leads us to conflict. My recovery has been a very long exploration of what I learned in my childhood. As I grew up, I acquired my workaholism, my perfectionism, and my desire to people-please others. In response to frustration of my need for acceptance, I had either exploded in a rage or imploded into a chemically-induced escape. This syndrome or reaction that is common in our culture has been dubbed "co-dependency" because there are two or more people dependent on each other to maintain a sense of order and control. They have the compulsion to control each other's behavior based on distrust. They can each clearly see the other's addictive, dysfunctional behavior and are blind to their own. This produces revolving cycles of conflict.

Blame carries with it an assumption that those being blamed will not change their behavior. Blame keeps the situation static. We get depressed, angry, and see ourselves as victims of a world gone wrong. This inhibits our ability to respond creatively, and we actually become part of the problem. When we get stuck on viewing war or violence as overwhelming problems, we become a victim of them.

I feel a deep despair sometimes about the future threats that my family is facing. There is a fear, a hidden panic, an anxiety-filled darkness, an exhausted waiting for the dawn with that wordless question: what's next? What sociopath will burst upon us with guns, bombs or poison?

It's the craziness of the world that drives us to become sane. It's the darkness that allows us to see the stars. Are we strong enough to really look deeply at the problem of violence in our world? Can we set ourselves free from blame?

We all seem to know what it is that we do *not* want. Our despair is based on the deep knowledge that we could do better. We know there could be another way. What would happen if we decided to reach for the stars, discover our own innate ability to be honest and humble?

We must be, and we can be, just as accountable as those we demand accountability from. Accountability is more compassionate and creative when it extends in all directions. We must inventory all our behaviors, not just *our* good points and *their* bad points, but both good and bad for everybody. When we have the attitude that everyone has something to contribute, then dialog will create the opportunity for change.

Do not blame war on the oil companies if you have bought their oil either directly for your own transportation, or indirectly through plastics, pharmaceuticals, fertilizer, or the fuel for distributing the products that support your lifestyle.

Do not blame the military-industrial complex if you have paid the taxes that funded them.

Do not blame the religious right if you have not strengthened your own spiritual path, joined a community and emboldened your leadership to take a stand.

Do not blame the Republicans, the neo-cons, or the Democrats if you have not engaged your neighbors, your local ward precinct, or your member of Congress in meaningful conversation.

Do not blame violence on the media if you are still paying attention to their view of reality and choosing to be depressed.

Do not expect our government to change its foreign and domestic policies of domination until *we* begin to see every human being, at all levels of our society, including those in the government, as equal to ourselves -- *totally equal!*

Do not expect the manipulation of fear to end until we become fearless, transcending the petty fears and illusions that separate us from each other. At the level of fear, we are all equal. As I worked Step 5, I became aware of how much I am beset with the same fears that affect everyone else. When these fears were shared in meetings the relief of tension would come in outbursts of laughter. Our shared nightmares became the paper tigers they really were. Without an outside viewpoint to our troubles, we can continue to lie to ourselves about how enormous they are.

Sometimes I wept for all the alienation I had imposed on my relationships needlessly. Sometimes I wept for the joy of knowing that the war within me was ending. I felt glad that I had pushed through the difficulty of facing my self-pity to see myself more realistically as an unfinished project. As I gained some self-forgiveness for myself, it extended to others. I became much more humble, tender, loving and compassionate toward other people. I discovered that I no longer need to demand that others be responsible for my feeling loved, supported and safe. I need to see me as lovable and capable of providing my own security in ways that don't conflict with others' needs to feel loved, supported and safe.

Relax

Working these steps allows us to see ourselves as children of the same human family of hurt and quarrel, and to see that we are all in the process of growing up to be mature and responsible adults. As we build our faith in this process, tensions relax and we feel expectant of a better life. Feelings of abandonment can begin to subside. Judgment and irritation can melt into light-hearted banter.

As I worked Step Six, I faced my impatience to free myself immediately from all of my hurt and disappointment, forever. However, if I looked at the many small steps I had made, I actually felt glimpses of joy, awe and wonder at how good life could really be. I felt grateful. I slowed down. I saw myself involved in a long process of slow changes that would accumulate over time. I didn't need to push the river. I could swim in it.

Of course, I still felt some anxiety about letting go completely. What would happen if I stopped struggling even more than I had already? Would life unravel into chaos? Looking back at these questions now, they seem amusing, considering how much chaos I had created with my constant, bitter struggling prior to recovery.

There was nothing I could actively do about my anxieties other than to remember how unreal they were. In those moments I could mentally switch channels to feelings of acceptance of the learning process which was leading me to serenity. Growing up, even at mid-life, became my highest priority.

Steps 7 - 9: Repair the damage

7. In a spirit of humility and compassion for yourself and all others, seek spiritual guidance in confronting your shortcomings which may contribute to conflict and emotional or physical violence.

8. Make a list of all persons you have harmed and become willing to make direct amends to all such people wherever possible, except when to do so would injure them or others.

9. Continue to be mindful of your actions and their effect on others, and when you have offended another, whether intentionally or not, promptly admit it and apologize.

Steps Seven through Nine follow the self-acceptance of the previous steps with actions that build the integrity that we had lost. The focus is upon choosing new behaviors that are congruent with our highest values. Honesty and transparency become important replacements to the pride and isolation of our prior lives. We can relax into asking for and accepting help with making changes in our behavior. We can melt into a sense of belonging to the rest of humanity. We become rich in our relationships.

I was not ready to rebuild my relationships until I had nine years of recovery. That may seem like slow progress. However, I had practiced damaging my relationships for about 40 years. Before I could even think about confronting that history, I had to witness other people in 12-step meetings model how to do it. They showed me how to listen, how to speak honestly about oneself, and how to ask for help. In addition, I needed to have the long perspective on the origins of my addictive behaviors in my childhood, and how many generations of dysfunctional parenting had set me up. I needed time to grieve the absence of a stable, nurturing, secure home and the resulting loss of my feelings, trust and playfulness. I had to see the fear of abandonment that prevented me from seeking an intimate relationship beyond the immediate gratification of lust. Most of all, I had to let go of the arrogance of believing that I should and could be the only one to repair myself.

Asking a higher power for help with my own transformation in Step Seven requires even greater humility and trust than I needed to pass the hurdle of Step Three. Fortunately, by working the steps in order, I had some practice in seeking spiritual help and a little more patience in waiting for an answer. I had developed some sense of how I fit within an unimaginably large and slow-moving system that required me to pay close attention to my style of interaction with it if I wanted any peace in my life. Prayer became a way for me to slow down, get some perspective and discover the benefits of not rushing into action. For example, one night when I couldn't sleep because I was worried about someone else's crazy behavior, I fell asleep by reciting the Serenity Prayer, *"God, grant me the serenity to accept the things I cannot change, the courage to change the things I can, and the wisdom to know the difference."*

Serenity didn't always come easily. I could not make Michael, age 5, go to sleep or stay in his bed at night, so I exploded once in anger, picked him up and threw him back onto his bed. I even held my hand over his mouth to muffle his hollering. Of course, the next day Michael avoided me and I felt very guilty. I was frustrated with myself for my failure to live up to my values. By working with my sponsor I eventually saw that I could change my reaction to the interruptions of my sleep by being more calm and nurturing. Instead of enforcing rules with anger and impatience, I could elicit my son's cooperation with my needs by modeling a peaceful and loving attitude.

I developed a more relaxed way of looking at tasks and goals so that I could be less demanding of myself and others. Instant gratification was no longer an option when I saw that it didn't meet my real needs. I became aware that slowing down to take care of my physical, mental, emotional and spiritual health was essential to repairing the damage I had done to myself and everyone around me.

I began making amends to myself by changing my behavior. I used acupuncture and a naturopath to heal sinus infections, shoulder bursitis, and skin fungus problems. I also got support from a process-oriented psychologist. I learned about taking care of myself in small ways and keeping things simple, such as not overeating sweets or overspending on credit. I no longer had to push myself beyond a reasonable balance of work and rest, and so I took a serious look at how I had become over-extended in my job.

I had learned all the technical skills of being a drug and alcohol counselor and passed the state certification test. However, because I had inappropriate empathy with the struggles of addicts, I would feel overly responsible for their recovery. This would place a limit on my effectiveness as a counselor. If one of my clients was describing an incident in which they had smoked some hash, I would literally salivate. If they described their impulse to commit suicide, I was right there with them. After four years of doing this, I was emotionally exhausted by my attempts to control and repress my feelings. I went back to the more manageable position of working with customers at a photo lab. I was much happier. I was pulling away from my workaholism and my desire to fix other people. I didn't have to change my customers' personalities in order to help them get better photographs. I could be friendly, and I could sleep better at night.

Step Eight came with some dread of the guilt about the harm I had done to other people.

I knew I had wronged so many and in so many ways, by being physically rough, by packing resentments, by refusing to help, by being financially irresponsible, by using sex and money as a substitute for love, and a long list of crimes of arrogance, intimidation, dishonesty, blame, gluttony and hatred. Step Eight also promised that I had a pro-active means to set myself free. In making amends we discover our ability not to undo the past, but to create a new future. At first I had my doubts that I could do this. My guilt and shame were still powerful. I had to carefully rehearse what I would say and ask my sponsor for his feedback before I attempted to make amends. I thought I might be ineffective, misunderstood or, because my habits were so strong, I might still repeat the same damaging behavior.

However, the effect upon me of doing this practice again and again was nothing short of miraculous as I gained the ability to look at myself as a mixture of mistakes and good intentions. I was not a permanently bad person. I could apologize for my mistakes. However, that by itself does not repair the damage. I must choose a different way of relating to people. The amends of Step Eight is the new behavior which heals resentments and overcomes isolation.

Most amends are not quick and easy. It took over two years to rebuild trust between myself and Valerie, even though our history of abuse and disrespect had been built over the course of only four years

For an example of a new behavior, I had an argument with a neighbor about some noise, and a conflict with Valerie over housekeeping duties. I turned the situations around by humbly and honestly describing to them how I had set myself up to be their opponent. I admitted to feeling self-righteous. Doing so set me free of feeling guilty (resentment of myself) because I owned my part in the conflict, and free from resentment of them because I could see their need for my help. My willingness to be honest gave the opportunity to my neighbor and my wife to also admit their part in creating the arguments. Immediately, we became partners in seeking a solution that worked for both of us. The alienation from each other that we were feeling was dissolved, we felt closer.

Perhaps one of my most powerfully effective amends has been the letter that I wrote to my father, who had been physically out of my life for over 45 years. However, he was still with me as the critical, punishing parental voice in my head. I wrote a letter of apology in which I took responsibility for being neither the child nor the adult that he would have had me be, for not having the manly courage to take life as it came, for choosing drugs and alcohol as a substitute for life. I forgave him for all the whippings and told him I understood why he had been so angry. I could still love my father, the human being inside the scary behavior, and I regretted so much that we had become enemies. I wept profusely, and sent it to the caretaker of the cemetery where he lay buried, asking them to burn the letter on his grave. The memory of this letter still brings tears to my eyes.

When I made amends to my father, I had no idea that I would then become the kind of adult that he would probably admire and be proud. The letter initiated a miracle of freedom to become my own person, accountable only to myself and not to what Daddy would have me do or be. I have finally become my own best, nurturing parent, a really good friend to myself. I have permission to be wrong, to make mistakes, to fall down and just get up again, to keep going strong. I can laugh at myself. In fact, being a bit foolish recently became one of my personal goals as a way of letting go of my perfectionism. I can be happy without being right, better, smarter, stronger or even good-looking. I have permission to be a fool.

When I see myself as fallible, that perception allows me to discover new behavior more easily. Without that self-forgiveness, I will

continue to sabotage my relationships and my life because I see myself as defective, a mistake. Instead of labeling myself as a passive-aggressive person, for example, I can simply acknowledge that I have routinely indulged in passive-aggressive behavior, see that clearly as a poor choice that I made, and look for a better alternative.

The ripple effect of the amends with my father is ongoing, repeating in waves of additional acts of letting go. I was once deflated by my sponsor's suggestion that I include *everyone* with whom I have a relationship on my amends list. Soon I saw his point. My character defects had affected everybody, sometimes more by resentful thoughts and acts of omission than by open conflicts. I could be a hazard to the people around me simply by hanging on to old hurts.

It wasn't until I had been in recovery for 20 years that I saw how I had made a lifestyle decision to abuse those in positions of power and authority such as teachers, police, or the entire federal government because of my history with my father. I would focus on listing their faults and attempt to steal or subvert their power. I no longer fear authority figures today. I can see the lovable human within the sometimes odious role they play.

Financial restitution was part of my amends to Barbara, my ex-wife. Many years after our divorce I repaid thousands of dollars in child support which I had pledged but failed to pay. Although this was important to my sense of integrity, I believe what has mattered more to her has been the restoration of our friendship, trust, and teamwork. Our negotiations about timing and place of visits from the grandchildren have worked out remarkably well. I respect her ability as a writer enough to ask for her guidance in writing this book, and she told me recently I rock as a peacebuilder. These are living amends, the return to relationship health on a daily basis.

The Ninth Step asks that we pay attention to the daily wanderings away from integrity in our relationships that may occur. I am vulnerable to falling asleep in this department by having an angry thought or speech, slipping into sarcasm, looking at a woman as a sex object, neglecting to send a birthday card, becoming irritable because I stayed up too late at night, rebelling against asking for help, giving people advice when they didn't ask for it, over-reacting to other drivers on the road when I'm the one who is speeding -- the list can be quite long!

However, once I develop the habit of watching what I am doing from the point of view of a compassionate friend, I can feel amused by the differences between the effects of my actions and the need they were attempting to fill. I can ask myself, "How's that working for you?" and laugh. The more that I do this, the more quickly do I recognize and intervene on the old behavior patterns that don't work any longer.

The pleasure and satisfaction of making small changes constantly over a long period of time becomes very rewarding, and eventually we gain the ability to stop a thought from becoming an action. At this level we re-awaken not only our own integrity, living true to our values, we find that our highest value is our ability to connect with our fellow human beings. We feel more alive, more healthy and more inspired when we are fully engaged in many friendships.

Without partnerships, relationships of unity and collaboration, we become spiritually poor. Material wealth, the accumulation of money, is often a sign of this kind of poverty. Money is a symbol of the human energy used to extract a resource or perform a service and as a symbol it is inert, the feces-trail of an energy exchange that has passed on. Having a great deal of money is like having a large pile of manure. It smells bad because at the core of our being, at the spiritual level, we know that all of the energy that we have ever received over our entire life was a gift, freely given without conditions. Why should we hang on to it? The sun gives life to all the plants, animals, and ourselves. Nobody owns the sun, it gives energy equally to all and demands nothing in return.

How we give ourselves away, how we use our energy in relationship with others, determines our true wealth. That gifting energy only has value when it is alive and moving in a particular moment of exchange. It cannot be stored, preserved, or manipulated into something greater.

However, there is an important side effect, a benefit which feeds back into the giving process, just like interest on a bank account. My experience of serenity and satisfaction has become more unshakable in direct correlation with the growth of my investment in family and friends. In recovery my wealth of relationships has multiplied exponentially in quantity and quality. I have invested more than I ever thought I possibly could in time, energy, and money into working for peace with other people. As this work accumulated benefits to my emotional life, the boundaries of the group that I consider to be family has included almost everyone that I encounter. Of course, there are always a few people that challenge me to stretch even further. Ultimately, the nearly 7 billion people on this planet that I will never meet become my extended family.

Steps 10 - 12: Find your response-ability

10. *Seek through prayer, meditation, and other self-care techniques, to gain emotional and spiritual strength (in the context of your specific religious or secular tradition).*

11. *Forgive those who may have offended you. Don't take things too personally. Remember that most people don't mean to offend, but that their actions (and yours) frequently lead to unintended negative consequences.*

12. *Commit to being an instrument of peace and healing among all those who cross your path in your life's journey. Don't hang onto resentment and anger. Let it go. Remember, the one who benefits the most from forgiveness is the person who gives it. It can bring a renewed sense of freedom and energy to your life.*

I have placed on the next page my summary graph of the evolution of a culture of violence to a culture of peace, based on Laszlo's model of organic transformation (p. 20). There are labels identifying personal traits attached to the highs and lows selected somewhat arbitrarily from many possible descriptors of the cultures of violence and peace. Fortunately, perhaps a hundred million people or more on the planet, according to Paul Ray and Sherry Anderson, authors of *The Cultural Creatives*,[31] are on the upward slope of the return to stability. However few they may be in number, they're growing in numbers quickly, they are strong, they have a vision of the promised land, and most important of all, they have *hope* because they survived

hitting bottom. They went off the cliff and bounced. They have uncovered their deepest feelings and released them.

To me, this is the real meaning of the word responsibility, the combination of two words, "response" and "ability." We all have this ability to respond to change, to adapt, to grow, and it is in this ability that we find our most human qualities. When we forgive ourselves for being unable to respond, we discover we *can* respond. The word "responsibility" is often used in the phrase "taking responsibility" or "assuming responsibility," with the meaning of accepting blame and the heroic duty to repair whatever is wrong. This way of thinking can cause us to take on overwhelming problems and feel totally stuck.

On the other hand, if we think of ourselves as *"giving* response-ability" from our innate talents and abilities, then a whole new range of options open up for us, and we can flow into solutions that were otherwise impossible. When we move out of the despair within ourselves, we end the cycle of addictive behaviors. When I change my inner world, my external behavior shifts to match, and I become a creative source of systemic change.

> *"We are all meant to shine, as children do..... It's not just in some of us; it's in everyone. And as we let our own light shine, we unconsciously give other people permission to do the same. As we are liberated from our own fear, our presence automatically liberates others."* [32]

Hope is the most valuable, most powerful catalyst that we can give to suicidal people, and what, I ask you, could be more

---

[31] Ray, P. & Anderson, S., The Cultural Creatives, Harmony Books, 2000.

[32] Williamson, M., A Return to Love, Harper Paperbacks, 1996

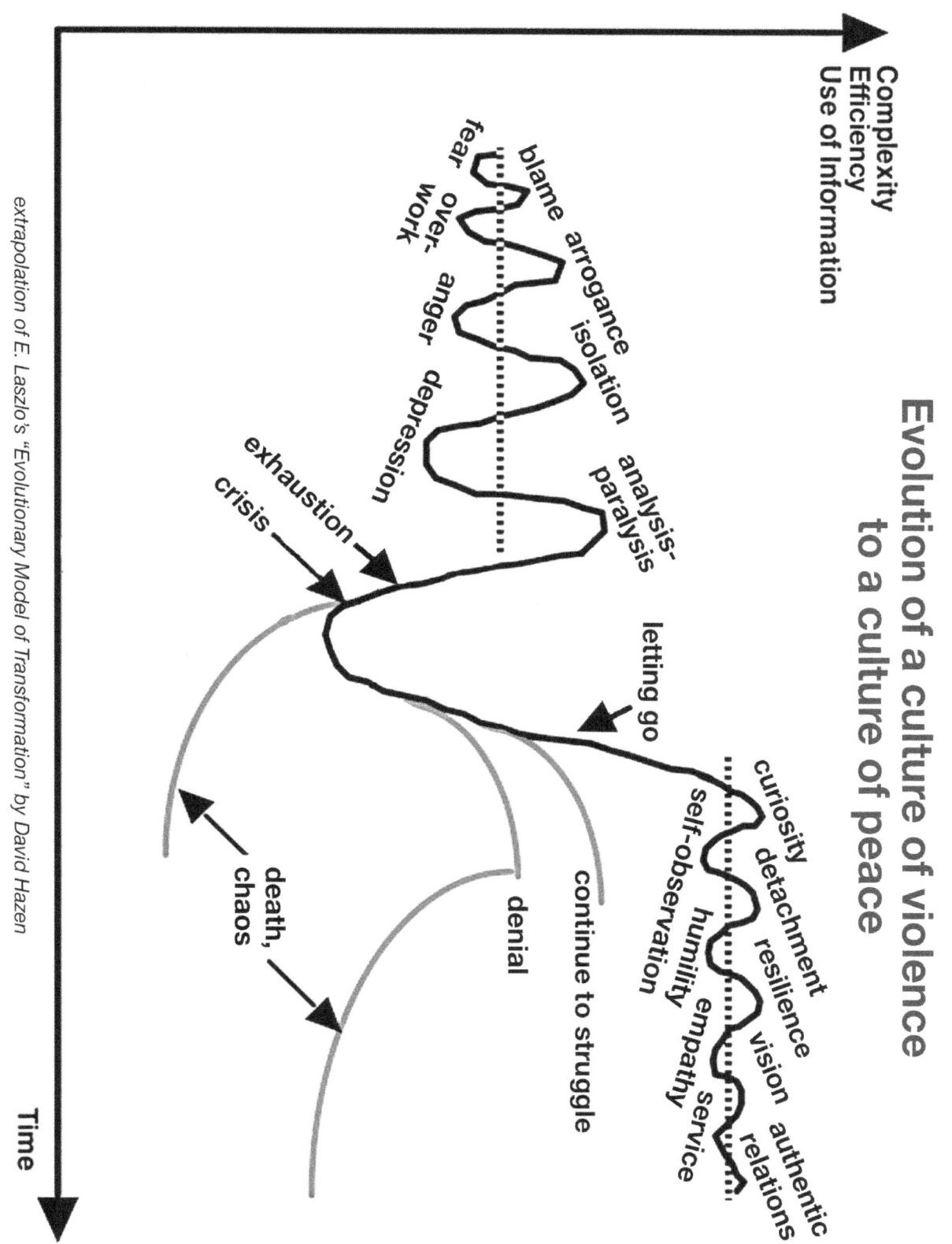

Evolution of a culture of violence to a culture of peace

Complexity
Efficiency
Use of Information

Time

extrapolation of E. Laszlo's "Evolutionary Model of Transformation" by David Hazen

fear
over-work
blame
arrogance
isolation
anger
depression
analysis-paralysis
exhaustion
crisis
letting go
continue to struggle
denial
death, chaos
curiosity
detachment
resilience
vision
authentic relations
service
empathy
humility
self-observation

suicidal than the culture in which we live?

The cultural creatives on the up-slope are no longer focusing on what horror awaits their failure, they give thanks for each new opportunity to set things right, and their positive expectations create a feedback loop where things *do* become right. They are resourceful, creative, and optimistic. Problems are reframed as opportunities to discover new and exciting resources and ideas in partnership with others. Life becomes a joyous adventure, and the goal is to be fully *alive*. The future belongs to them, and they are calling *"YOOHOO!"* to the rest of humanity. When we move out of the despair within ourselves, we end the power of the domination and violence paradigm immediately. We are free! Unfortunately, we are also as fragile as newborn babies, and mutual support from others like ourselves is critical.

I believe we are here to free others, and this happens naturally as we regain our feelings that were once frozen. Part of being fully human is to be in community with those who share in the same struggle, to be in full, honest and open communication about our feelings. Because we are human, we are prone to forget who we are, who we are with, who we belong to, and where we are going. We need each other to remind ourselves of those things. This needs to happen on a daily basis, as a discipline, as part of a new lifestyle that we adopt for ourselves. This is what I believe Gandhi meant when he said *"We must be the change we wish to see."* We must become the beloved community and accept it as the destiny for all of humanity.

What is our personal ability to respond to the culture of violence? Peace can arise when we no longer focus on the differences between "us" and "them," and we discover the commonalities among us. For example, I share the anger, grief and cynicism of everyone who believes peace is impossible, *and* I believe that we also have in common a deep longing for it.

This focus is extremely powerful. I am willing to expose myself to the pain of learning how to remain in the conversation about building a world that meets everyone's needs, instead of shutting down or lashing out to gain control by claiming to be right. This willingness, this hope for a better world, comes from a belief in the basic goodness of others and creates the space for forgiveness.

When we pause the action to attend to our feelings, others' feelings, nature and the Universe, our fear of abandonment will dissolve. We will truly be free from the paradox of attacking the people, animals, and environment that we truly love. After all, at the end of the day, is not the stated purpose of domination, aggression and violence to resolve a conflict and return to a state of relative harmony? I say "relative" because we know that post-violence harmony is unstable and unsustainable.

Stable harmony and peace come from security, health and growth for all people. It is not a static destination. It is not the end of conflict. It is a dynamic stability very much like balancing a bicycle in motion, a skill that may be tricky to learn at first. Peace is a never-ending process of recovery from domination and violence. This is how I understand and speak about peace, as an active story in which we participate, labor and toil. Peace -- a sustainable world -- is many acts of inner transformation, daily actions of acceptance, release of subjective judgments and continuous collaboration.

We live in a time of rapid change, when it has become more obvious with every passing day that seeking power over others through aggression wastes energy and produces repeating struggles. Nothing is now more important than breaking the cycle of violence by learning how to create the joy, wonder and power of people who listen to each other, deeply, and then collaborate together in community. Real freedom from violence comes from doing the difficult work of learning to listen, a passive response that is often considered to be the opposite of what is needed. Yet throwing ourselves into action, struggling to resolve conflict with active strategies, is exhausting precisely because it is disconnected from the whole truth of the situation. Something is missing because we have not heard the others involved.

I am going to say that what is missing is non-verbal heart knowledge. Other words might be used, such as intuition, spiritual sensitivity, a whole-systems perspective, clarity about the meaning or purpose of one's life, awareness of transcendent values, connection to what is alive in ourselves, humility in the face of the unknown, communion with the Ultimate Reality or God, or simply linking head, heart, and body together to reach one's full potential as a human being. These words describe something that is for most people very intangible, mysterious, and outside the grasp of scientific testing. The word *mysticism* is used to describe this experience of a state of consciousness or knowledge that is beyond normal human sensory perceptions or description.

All the world's religions were established from the teachings of mystics, including Buddha, Jesus, Lao Tze, Abraham, Krishna and Mohammed. In spite of the distortions introduced to those religions by later people who didn't trust mysticism, I see that the original, common purpose of religions and spiritual disciplines is to make heart knowledge a tangible and reproducible experience so that it can be included in our strategies for resolving conflicts. Heart knowledge is then expressed as the practice of empathy and compassion for the creation of a state of harmony and well-being. So, no matter how one is engaged in this pursuit of harmony, formally or informally, the essential ingredient is mysticism.

As a child I had no conscious mystical experiences that I remember. I was required by my parents to attend Christian churches. The most nearly-mystical experience I had was in Minneapolis at the age of ten, singing Latin Christmas carols in a choir in a gothic stone cathedral that had a magnificent pipe organ. That was very uplifting.

However, I abandoned organized religion as a crude invention of men and not of God about the time I began using alcohol and drugs at the age of 19. I became agnostic. I didn't pray and I knew nothing of empathy and compassion, neither for myself nor others.

Then for the last 15 years of my active addiction, I began seeking psychological and spiritual answers to my persistent life problems. I developed a strong interest in mysticism and participated in many trainings for human potential and esoteric knowledge. I developed a meditation practice and then abandoned it when I entered recovery. I had proven to myself that it didn't make me happy, quell my anger, or change my behavior. It certainly did not seem like the path to enlightenment that I thought it would be. It took a long time, later in recovery, for me to begin new experiments in meditation.

The experiments were always done in response to stress, when I was desperate for a way to calm down. When I got involved with careless spending, overeating, perfectionism or resentments, I would spin out of balance, grasping for control over my life. I would lose my emotional sobriety in the childish fear that I was once again alone and without the strength or ability to respond to the demands of life. My low self-esteem was getting in the way. I believed that to be in a spiritual relationship, I needed to *do* more, be more *in control*, have the *right* answers, or in some way prove that I was worthy.

In a similar way with prayer, I made several small requests for help during my first years of recovery. They were always short prayers, like baby steps. Sometimes I would simply say "hello" to God if I was watching a beautiful sunset or autumn colors, or eating an especially delicious meal, or drifting off to sleep. Gradually, my prayers increased in frequency and sincerity as I gained some confidence that they might be getting some answers. I started to walk with more heart knowledge and spiritual strength.

Through prayer and meditation I opened myself to receiving the small nudges of support to be a better husband, father and productive member of society. One day I spontaneously stopped to help a stalled motorist, a situation I would have previously passed by without a second thought. I pulled him out of a busy intersection and gave him a jump start. For a moment, I was no longer thinking of myself as unworthy. I was starting to act as if I were worthy of spiritual guidance.

In my eighth year of recovery, I was very much challenged to find my ability to respond to the loss of yet another job. I had been working at a treatment center which had become financially insolvent, and as the last days of work approached, I became moody and irritable. I seemed unable to become an acknowledged and rewarded professional in a successful career. I felt self-pity for my chronic inability to market myself. I also blamed this employer for their weaknesses in leadership and planning. I saw that I had become too reliant upon them for holding up my self-esteem. My impulse was to repress my feelings of grief and anxiety, and so I remained stuck, unable to relax. I didn't want to admit that I was feeling weak, frightened, or vulnerable. Instead, I had angry outbursts at Michael and blamed Valerie for my defensiveness. I also scraped my knee open and bleeding, not just once, but *three* times.

So I had to stop, pray, meditate, and take my own inventory. I saw there was some forgiving for me to do and amends to make. I had to forgive the employer, forgive myself, and forgive Michael and Valerie. I began to see how I had allowed fear to grip my thoughts, as it had done most of my life. Once I got more perspective on what I had done to myself, I could see that I had a choice. I had the opportunity to take care of myself better, to open the dark corners of my heart to other people, admit my faults and ask for help. I could take the risk to be honest. I wrote in my journal that the value of learning from the stresses in my life "far outweighs the painful experience of letting old pain surface."

The crisis of losing my job then became a gift in which I gained a closeness and trust with not only my higher power but also the people around me. I felt warm, relaxed, adventurous, excited by and interested in my life. I felt renewed, which is what a spiritual awakening is all about -- coming alive again, remembering that the deep well of joy within us comes not from sensory pleasures but from a heart knowledge of our connection to an indestructible source of support.

Catching a glimpse of wildness

To me the essence of spirituality or heart knowledge is listening. The heart, the small voice, whatever you wish to call it, is constantly transmitting its messages. Are we listening? Do we even hear? If we are to escape the obsession for control of what appear to be threatening situations, we need a conscious practice of listening not only to ourselves, but to the heart messages we receive from others. What we hear is the basis of our natural ability to respond. Most of us already listen to a certain degree. Our relationships would not exist at all if we did not listen. If we were to greatly intensify our willingness to listen and develop our skill in listening we would greatly affect the level of intimacy, trust and security (which is peace) that we feel.

As we sharpen our listening to drink of this well of wisdom that seems to come from nowhere, we are faced with the need to still the noisy chatter of our own minds, to get out of our own way, to let the final evaporation of our ego take place. When we master the ability to focus elsewhere than on the fears, the judgments, the opinions, the analysis, the stories -- the information overload -- then like a small child we can be totally immersed in what is happening in the present moment. We can respond with the totality of our nervous system, which contains vast amounts of activity outside the verbal content of our brains. We can respond to the synapses around our heart, which have been shown to be among the most sensitive in our bodies to events occurring far beyond the reach of our other senses.[33]

When we are listening this deeply, we are able to catch those "glimpses of wildness," the source of our aliveness, or as some may say, our soul. Some people may refer to this mental state in which we have literally stepped outside of our own mind as meditation, and for other people it may be described as a kind of "high" they experience as the result of balancing their brain chemistry with focused physical activities such as dancing or long-distance running. Although the consumption of mood-altering chemicals can also produce a similar experience, substituting chemicals for a natural ability that we all possess makes that ability less available to us when we most need it, when we are under stress.

It is said that the only constant in the universe is change, and we literally have a choice to respond to change with pleasure, delight and wonder, or to respond with the pain we call stress, the resistance to change. Meditation in all of its many varieties gives us the opportunity to choose the former and live our lives from a place of calm observation, detached from the drama of what happened

yesterday and what might happen tomorrow, the changes that swirl around us. Meditation can be as formal as sitting in certain ways or as informal as a walk in the woods. The martial arts, especially the more ancient ones such as Tai Chi or Qi Gong, are somewhere in between active and passive, a moving meditation. Meditation can be religious or secular. There is no one way to do it that works for everybody, and it is important to find a practice that works for you and then exercise that practice to build the skill as if it were a muscle. The human psyche contains a natural state of meditation at birth which is quickly obscured by modern culture, and it takes practice to regain and remember this talent.

There are a bewildering number of choices if you wish to learn a meditation technique, and if you haven't found one that calls to you, I suggest you try Open Focus[34] as a starting point. I have been practicing these meditations for about three years. There is no religious dogma attached to it. It is completely secular and derived from brain-wave research. Thirty-five years ago I learned various meditation techniques from the Arica school, and when I added Open Focus to my repertoire it made my practice much more enjoyable and rewarding. My very first experiences took me to a deep presence of mind I had not experienced before in my other practices. I've been delighted to observe how, later in my day, I've been able to call upon this state of mind to relieve stress, interrupt obsessive thoughts, and allow creative ideas to flourish. I've been very enthusiastic about sharing Open Focus with anyone!

To possess the talent of meditation is one of the most exhilarating freedoms, the greatest fun, I believe, that we can ever know as human beings. This is why I make the claim that letting

[33] Surel, D., *Speaking from the Heart*, EDGESCIENCE #6, 2011

[34] See Fehmi & Robbins, *The Open Focus Brain*, Trumpeter, 2008.

old vanity evaporate, L.O.V.E., is the only law or rule of behavior that I need to constantly observe and remember. The experience of freedom derives from the knowledge that the still, small voice deep within us is permanent and indestructible, always available whenever we need it, regardless of what is going on around us in our daily lives.

When we become aware of our own, permanent consciousness we begin to "see as God sees." Gratitude flows naturally as we allow ourselves to be tools of co-creation. Our consciousness is a gift to us that we did not create and for which we are the stewards. It came as part of the package of this life, and gives us reason to believe that there might be a great source of energy and power, much greater than our own, that we can rely on. I feel secure in the knowledge that I have not been abandoned by this source. That security creates in me the feeling of being beloved, so I can call it love, and I can give up struggling.

When I feel beloved, when I feel secure, when I feel free, not only do I feel very excited to be alive, I am able to be forgiving and understanding with my fellow human beings. I become aware of *their* permanent, indestructible, still, small voice that is speaking to them in *their* language. This is why I make the claim that when I let my old vanity evaporate I become aware of love incarnate victorious everywhere, A.L.I.V.E.

Because I am a vulnerable human being prone to hang onto my cultural conditioning for a sense of safety, I need frequent reminders that a greater and more sustainable refuge exists outside of my culture, beyond any religion, politics, or science. Meditation is my touchstone to that limitless energy outside my small self.

I make a practice of prayer and meditation every morning immediately after I get out of bed, unless I've slept in late, beyond 7 AM for some reason, or I'm traveling. I have an altar space set up in the corner of my study. This space is my spiritual "home." I have not publicly shared the details of my meditation because I don't wish comparisons made to what may seem to be a highly unorthodox routine. It nourishes me. It may not nourish you. I share it now to encourage you to create your own unorthodox routine that speaks to your heart.

I begin with a salutation to the infinite, "OM," and then slowly and deliberately recite three prayers, focusing on the meaning of the words. I begin with the Prayer of Abandonment by Charles de Foucauld (1858-1916). I like to address the Creator in Aramaic, the language of Jesus, as *"Abwoon,"* which has multiple meanings beyond the literal and usual translation of "Father." For me it invokes an awareness of the unity of energy flowing throughout the macrocosm of the Universe and within the microcosm of myself.

> *Abwoon, into Thy hands I abandon myself.*
> *Do with me whatever you will and whatever you do I will thank you and remain always grateful.*
> *Let Thy will be done in me as in all your creatures.*
> *Into Thy hands I commend my spirit.*
> *I give it to you with all the love in my heart, for I love you, Lord, and so long to give myself with a trust beyond all measure.*
> *Amen.*

My second prayer is my version of the Lord's Prayer. I had known the words of this prayer since I was a child, and had been reciting it for years without ever pausing to wonder what it really meant. One day, I wanted to deeply absorb the original intent of the prayer, so I took each line and wrote what the words meant to me personally, what my heart wanted to be saying to God. Later on, I found a translation from the

Aramaic language by Neil Douglas-Klotz[35], and discovered that the flexibility of translation could include the words I had written.

O, Holy One,
All of your creation is sacred and alive with your Spirit.
May your Divine Consciousness awaken in all of us,
May your Divine Will be done through all of us.
Grant us spiritual strength and understanding for this day.
Help us to accept ourselves as we are and to accept others as our brothers and sisters.
Keep us focused on feeling Your Love in our hearts, so there is no room for fear.
We are always in Your care, for You are eternal, our source and our destination.
Amen.

My third prayer is an extended version of the Serenity Prayer, which has been passed on for centuries from an unknown author.

Mother-Father God, grant me the serenity to accept the things that I cannot change, the courage to change the things that I can, and the wisdom to know the difference.
Grant me patience for the changes that take time, appreciation for all that I have, and tolerance (or empathy and compassion) for those with different struggles.
Amen.

For the next 30 or so minutes I then vary what I do, sometimes chanting, sometimes visualizing a sequence of glowing chakras (energy centers) followed by an imaginary journey to a place where I absorb the strength and potency of a mountain, the serenity and tranquility of a lake, and the splendor and vitality of a tree. Sometimes I have used a guided training session of Open Focus, and as I have developed that skill, I have been able to practice without the recording, simply resting in the silence. The deep peace I experience there now makes it unnecessary, even annoying, to use meditative music to enhance my practice.

I compare learning to meditate to learning to ride a bicycle, except that the dynamic tension between mind and heart is much more difficult to balance than a bicycle. It took years of steady practice for me to link together more than a few seconds of silence. Eventually, even the effort to maintain a chatter-free mind lost its importance. Whatever my mind wants to do while I sit back and watch is fine with me. If I can simply remember from time to time that my internal witness has no opinion or judgment, no doubts about anything, and is completely at peace, I am happy.

Which brings me to my belief that all mysticism, all religion, and all spiritual practices including the 12-Step programs have the goal which is sometimes hidden, yet nevertheless is the goal, of building awareness of that internal witness that is free of conflict, free of violence, and is the source of peace and happiness.

We are all response-able

Meditation or introspection that merely resulted in "feeling good" about Love and Peace without authentic expression in committed action has become for me a feeling without

---

[35] Douglas-Klotz, N., *Prayers of the Cosmos*, HarperOne, 1993.

integrity. Andrew Harvey has said that there is no authentic spirituality without active, unceasing work for social justice[36], of which peace is the foremost precept.

> *"A spirituality that is only private and self-absorbed, one devoid of an authentic political and social consciousness, does little to halt the suicidal juggernaut of history. On the other hand, an activism that is not purified by profound spiritual and psychological self-awareness and rooted in divine truth, wisdom, and compassion will only perpetuate the problem it is trying to solve, however righteous its intentions. When, however, the deepest and most grounded spiritual vision is married to a practical and pragmatic drive to transform all existing political, economic, and social institutions, a holy force - the power of wisdom and love in action - is born. This force I define as Sacred Activism."*
> -- Andrew Harvey

My spirituality births my activism for peace by nurturing my sense of connection and healing my isolation. A few years ago, I had the conscious awareness that everything I think, feel, or do -- how I express who I truly Am -- affects not only my immediate relationships but also the history of humanity forever as those relationship interactions ripple forward in time. My first experience was a veritable Dark Night of the Soul, an incredible, unbearable grief for the damage that has been done to this planet and with which I have been inextricably complicit. I

became ready to devote my life to a world of non-violence.

I became ready to hear the still, small voice within me get my attention in a very dramatic way. I have shared this story with only a few close friends, and now feel it appropriate in the context of this book to share it more publicly. I had been practicing daily meditation and doing the Prayer of Abandonment for some length of time, I am not sure how long, when I had a sudden experience of being surrounded by fire during my meditation. I was frightened and immediately opened my eyes. A few weeks later, I had joined a weekend prayer retreat at a Catholic nunnery in Mount Angel, Oregon. During our first gathering as a group on Friday evening, we were being guided through a meditation when the fire surrounded me again, For some reason, I felt safer in allowing it to continue, which it did for several minutes.

It frightened me at first and then aroused my curiosity. This time, I was able to stay present and witness it. I had no idea what it meant until I left the room. As I walked out of the room my eyes landed on a folded origami crane. I suddenly was overwhelmed with yet another unexpected heart "message." I knew beyond a shadow of a doubt that I was here on earth to work on world peace. Several years later I heard Michael Meade explain how our life's journey is about remembering the agreement we made about our life's purpose before our consciousness became attached to our body.[37]

I could not accept this message, this remembering, this connecting of head and heart, at first. I wept. I argued with God for about a half-hour. Then I accepted that I didn't need to have the map of the entire journey, only the next most obvious step. I have become clear since this incident that the task of world peace is not

---

[36] http://www.andrewharvey.net/sacred_activism.php, also Harvey, The Hope: A Guide to Sacred Activism, Hay House 2009

[37] Meade, M., Fate and Destiny, Greenfire Press 2010.

my sole responsibility, either. This is a task for everyone.

Recovery has to be a social process. Accepting that we are not alone is the first, necessary step. I don't think anyone in our culture has escaped being traumatized as a victim, as a witness, or as a perpetrator of violence. The role of perpetrator as a soldier in war is perhaps the most traumatizing.[38] In order to harm other people, animals, or the natural environment we have to learn to deny our own humanity. When we do that, part of us dies inside. We become numb. Finding our way back to fully being alive requires support for the process of letting go of the familiar, and leaping into the unknown. We need a map and consistent pathway beacons, friends and mentors who remind us of the big picture, accept our wanderings, and celebrate our mileposts.

The feedback and encouragement from companions is crucial. The cultural norms of domination and violence were established by the behaviors of individuals repeated by generations over thousands of years. Leading by example, providing advice and discipline to their family and community, each individual contributed something to what has become "standard operating procedure" in response to conflict. The culture of domination is composed of many rules, beliefs and assumptions that are generally accepted and rarely questioned. They become automatic and unconscious. Because there are so very many cultural norms, it may take many generations to re-examine the ones that aren't working any longer and to establish new standards for the entire population of the planet. However, small groups of people who understand the need for a different kind of response to conflict can plant the seeds of new cultural norms. People in recovery groups often will refer to the outside culture as "the normies"

in order identify themselves as nonconformists and standard-bearers of a culture that has departed from the conventional way of doing things.

The process of social change requires each individual, then, to move through the fear, anger and grief around the loss of old ideas and familiar behaviors. We need the courage to act in spite of our fears, to not only repair the damage but also to prevent it from happening again, and we get this courage from each other. The ability to let go of our damaging behaviors, the ones that have harmed the people around us, depends upon our moving forward in small affinity groups of mutual support for that grieving process. As we practice giving away our compassion to each other around the issues that we share in common, we become internally balanced and secure. We find strengths we never knew we had, and virtue in the original sense of the Latin word, *virtus,* meaning "valor or courage."

Courage is important because the old habits are familiar, comfortable and difficult to escape. New habits seem very strange, uncomfortable, even dangerous. When we are re-programming the ideas we learn in childhood, we have to hold down the "on" button for the new programming to take effect, because the tendency to relapse is powerful. By talking about our fear with another human being, exposing our beliefs and assumptions to the light of examination, we rob them of their power. As I uncover my own fear, I see that I have the same ones as everybody else. Then I am at peace. I no longer have the tunnel vision of myself as a single particle separate from all other human beings.

I need to act as if this were true in order for it to actually become true. If I do not work the recovery process, if I do not live it and give

---

38 Grossman, D., On Killing: The Psychological Cost of Learning to Kill in War and Society, Little, Brown and Co, 1995

it away, I will lose it. I am busy being born and giving birth all at the same time. I need to practice empathy and compassion in the same way I need to practice any new skill I wish to learn. I am compelled to do this work of recovery from dependency on violence literally for my own survival, because I have become violent, understand violence from the inside and never want to go back to it. I need to strengthen my insights by sharing my story with others. Because my heart has broken open, I feel compelled to bring the world with me, for my own sake. Receiving empathy and compassion in safe group settings helps me identify these practices and motivates me to share them. The way out is the way through.

I look at the group process of Alcoholics Anonymous (AA) as a great example of how to establish new cultural norms. It has revolutionized the definition of alcoholics so that they are no longer regarded as permanently and morally corrupt or mentally ill but as sensitive, intelligent people diseased by a behavior that can be put in remission by education, mutual support and practice. As a result, millions of alcoholics are now sober.

The AA organization has also established new norms about the process of social change, demonstrating quickly on a large scale that a leaderless, egalitarian movement is very powerful and effective. That same structure is one of the ways in which nonviolence can be, and is being, introduced into our culture. As Martin Luther King, Jr. has noted, the nonviolent activists are "creatively maladjusted" to a sick society. They are not crazy or weak, they have a desperate need to escape the culture of domination. We can see this effort in the horizontal, family-like organizational structure being attempted by the Occupy movement.

This very perceptive statement by Stanley Hauerwas summarizes the importance of mutual support:

"I say I'm a pacifist because I'm a violent son of a bitch. I'm a Texan. I can feel it in every bone I've got. And I hate the language of pacifism because it's too passive. But by avowing it, I create expectations in others that hopefully will help me live faithfully to what I know is true but that I have no confidence in my own ability to live it at all. That's part of what nonviolence is -- the attempt to make our lives vulnerable to others in a way that we need one another. To be against war -- which is clearly violent -- is a good place to start. But you never know where the violence is in your own life. To say you're nonviolent is not some position of self-righteousness--you kill and I don't. It's rather to make your life available to others in a way that they can help you discover ways you're implicated in violence that you hadn't even noticed." [39]

So, when you or I adopt nonviolence as a principle or policy we cannot prevent ourselves from being transformed, in the same way that the entire lifestyle of an alcoholic changes when they adopt a policy of sobriety. The similarity of AA to activism for a culture of nonviolence is to me remarkable. Both movements rely on education, mutual support and practice, and both introduce new norms about what is and what is not healthy behavior. Alcoholism is a form of violence against oneself, so both movements have in common the impulse to recover from a life of violence. In addition, the mainstream

---

[39] McCarthy, C., "I'm a pacifist because I'm a violent son of a bitch," A profile of Stanley Hauerwas, The Progressive, April 1, 2003

culture will ridicule such nonconformist activity to preserve the existing norms of violence, so any recovery effort poses the risk of humiliation. Mutual encouragement is essential.

We all fear being exposed to potential humiliation. However, we cannot be humiliated if we are humble. What does this mean? When we review our personal history through a process like the *Twelve Steps of Personal Peacemaking,* we see how our low self-esteem and victim mentality developed into a violent lifestyle. We see our past, see it with grief and anger, see it mirrored in the people around us, see it in our culture, and then develop the courage to let go of the anger. The grieving for our past in the safe space of a group of like-minded people brings us to the doorstep of an entirely new way of being compassionate for ourselves and others. We can see that we did the best that we could with the resources available to us at the time, and now we are more free to choose different strategies. We become more accepting and forgiving of ourselves, less violent with ourselves. We also begin to suspend our judgment of other people, their life journeys or their particular way of disease and suffering.

How can we know what terrible pain will shape us into a being of inner beauty and courage?

How can we know on what crucible our souls will take shape and transcend the darkness that has embraced us? Or what fire we must walk through to find that Higher Power that can purge our being of the seductive seeds of destruction so that we may emerge whole and awake to see our true path.

How else can we recognize the shimmering dawn of hope unless we have wept tears of desolation?

When viewed that way, who is to say what is tragedy and what is good fortune?

All I know is that out of the fire of fear and despair has come a life worth living; a life that reflects the light of a soul redeemed to serve a Higher Power and shed light to others in a too often dark universe.
--- Leslie Habetler

Genuine and shared grief is important to the process of recovery from violence. Within the ashes of grief we find the acceptance and compassion which is the Truth-Force, or *satyagraha,* of a life of service to the transformation of humanity's addiction to violence. Humility is being able to say, "I belong here on this earth. Let there be peace on earth, and let it begin with me."

That spark of self-esteem and response-ability is the real beginning of recovery from violence dependency. As long as we focus on creating nurturing relationships, not run away from difficult emotions and will ourselves to be empathetic, present and grounded, there is no way that we can fail to attract the spiritually sick and tired into recovery from violence. Peace will then grow.

The small moments of compassion that represent internal transformations of individuals have an incremental effect. They cannot be underestimated as to their significance. Humanity has now arrived at a very powerful moment in our history when the transformation of a few is beginning to spread through our global electronic brain, the internet, like a virus to billions of interconnected neurons. The story of Eugene City of Peace illustrates how important the internet has become.

Gestation & birth of a City of Peace

When I left the National Peace Academy's[40] Peacebuilding Peacelearning Intensive in August of 2010, I felt that I and all the other participants had become "ordained" peacebuilders, that we were being sent forth on a sacred mission. For me, this has become my profession. I have no other work. I have been inspired to redouble my efforts to form collaborations and heart-to-heart connections.

Because I had previously been aware of The Shift Network's presence on the internet,[41] I heard an inspiring teleconference call about micro-finance during Peace Week[42] in September of that year. I began two initiatives to intervene on multi-generational poverty. One was to form a pool of investors for peer-to-peer lending at the local level on the model of Kiva.org.[43] After several meetings among several dozen interested people, we encountered legal and regulatory barriers to the idea. However, we discovered a way to crowd-source direct grants for social entrepreneurs through fundraising dinners.[44]

In addition, I saw the potential for those in poverty to either earn an income or feed themselves by planting potatoes in the leaves that normally get piled in the street during the fall and hauled away by the city. The idea caught on among several people associated with the Transition Town movement,[45] and we formed a team to find an unused alley for the planting. The potatoes were harvested recently and donated to Occupy Eugene. It wasn't a huge harvest, but the project received media coverage and inspired the local Mission to start their own "Peace Garden."

In November 2010, I inaugurated a Peacebuilder Community group to encourage skill-building for group sustainability, collaboration, and community-building. We found the most value in sharing the personal histories of our activism. This group met monthly for one year and has now merged with the Eugene City of Peace[46] group which has been linked with the International Cities of Peace[47] via the internet. The seed idea for a City of Peace in Eugene came from my association with the campaign for a U.S. Department of Peace, organized by The Peace Alliance.[48] From 2005 to 2011 I was the Oregon State Coordinator for that campaign, and then began to ask the question, what would a Department of Peace do if it had a local office in Eugene? We wanted to advocate for increased civic conversation as the path to peace.

I collaborated with other peace organizations in Eugene to inventory the more than 75 peace, justice, and sustainability

---

[40] http://www.nationalpeaceacademy.us

[41] http://theshiftnetwork.com

[42] http://peaceweek.info

[43] http://www.kiva.org

[44] http://sundaysoup.org/

[45] http://www.transitioneugene.org

[46] Google-search "Eugene City of Peace" for best results. It doesn't have its own domain name yet.

[47] http://www.internationalcitiesofpeace.org

[48] http://www.thepeacealliance.org/

organizations in our community. We sorted them into the seven areas of human security as defined by the United Nations.[49] I created a database of all their contact information that was then useful in drawing out 20 organizations and over 200 people for a Peace Feast and Walk on the anniversary of the Iraq war in March of 2011. The mayor spoke, the Samba percussion band led the walk, and we all ate chili and cornbread prepared by a marvelous team of volunteers from Church Women United.

In April, we began building a relationship with the Eugene Human Rights Commission by setting up an information table at a human rights summit. I met with their staff people to propose that the city conduct a Peace Index survey to establish a baseline for measuring progress. Recently, I was invited to join the University of Oregon's Center for Intercultural Dialogue to present the Charter for Compassion[50] for endorsement by the City. Implementing the Charter would require a diverse panel of citizens and would qualify the city to be a City of Compassion as well as an International City of Peace.

In May, the team that had been advocating for a U.S. Department of Peace shifted its focus to creating a Eugene City of Peace, and began a series of informal potluck dinners to build our social connection. In September, we collaborated with the local Sufi community to organize Dances of Universal Peace[51] for the International Day of Peace. In October, I was overwhelmed by the presentation of two awards from two local organizations in recognition for my peacebuilding efforts.

My greatest excitement, however, came on October 21, 2011, as I witnessed the birth of a beautiful child: a City of Peace. I was present when the Occupy Eugene protest organizers set up a liaison in response to a request from the police department. Since that meeting, the police had refrained from making any arrests for violation of the city's anti-camping ordinance and would continue to do so as long as the Occupy camp remained nonviolent and did not endanger the public. Then tensions suddenly arose over an executive order issued by the Eugene city manager asking the police to enforce the ordinance. The manager had probably received complaints about the encampment.

The day after the arrest order had been issued, a meeting was hurriedly scheduled. I found about it only 90 minutes in advance because I chanced upon comments posted online, on Facebook. I called my friends at Community Mediation Services to facilitate the discussion and provide a safe space for listening and sharing. They invited me to participate. I had very little time to get dressed and eat breakfast.

The conversation between Occupy Eugene, the city manager and the Police Department then went so well that the lawyer for the Occupiers thought she was dreaming! A spokeswoman of the homeless youth was incredibly eloquent. We met for two hours. The conversation was open, honest, and from the heart. Nobody was ever upset. Everyone had a chance to speak.

I spoke of my desire for win-win solutions that would be a model for other cities interested in positive community-police relations. I was floored when everyone agreed to work in good faith towards that! I felt this was a victory of the heart. I now have a vision for expanding this conversation city-wide and am in

---

49 http://en.wikipedia.org/wiki/Human_security#UNDP.27s_1994_definition

50 http://charterforcompassion.org

51 http://www.dancesofuniversalpeace.org

consultation with talented facilitators, a social media/nonviolent communication expert, and a resource person in empathy and compassion.

I am proud of this photo, taken on October 21 at the end of the conversation. Paul Simon is on the left, Eugene police Lieutenant Sam Kamkar is in the middle, and I am on the right. Paul, who was the Oregon Student Peace Alliance Coordinator for several years, worked closely with the Eugene Occupiers and is also committed to creating more inclusive community conversations. Lt. Kamkar was born in Iran and immigrated to the USA with his parents when he was just three years old. He is very supportive of the right to free speech, is the police liaison to the Occupy Eugene movement, and has a great sense of humor!

When there is enough "deep listening" to ourselves, each other, to nature and the Universe, the questions about how to achieve our goals -- what actions to take -- becomes an effortless dance. Perhaps in this time of crisis, we will finally be motivated to teach ourselves the lessons of nonviolence. It will take some time, some practice, some real effort, and genuine courage to do what we have never done before. All we need is the conviction, as it is so popular to say in political speech these days, that "We can do it," with the emphasis on we. Let's have a real, honest conversation about violence in our Earth community.

> *This is the true joy in life, being used for a purpose recognized by yourself as a mighty one. Being a force of nature instead of a feverish, selfish little clod of ailments and grievances, complaining that the world will not devote itself to making you happy. I am of the opinion that my life belongs to the whole community and as long as I live, it is my privilege to do for it what I can. I want to be thoroughly used up when I die, for the harder I work, the more I live. I rejoice in life for its own sake. Life is no brief candle to me. It is a sort of splendid torch which I have got hold of for the moment and I want to make it burn as brightly as possible before handing it on to future generations.*
> --- George Bernard Shaw

That I might be able to deliver hope to someone else is one of the most satisfying adventures of my life. My gift has been sharing my journey with you. I belong to you. I am grateful to have you in my life. *Ubuntu:* "I am what I am because of who we all are."

I have only skimmed some of the highlights of this return to some sanity in my life. I don't beat myself up much any more. I am not going to claim that I never get upset or angry, nor claim that I don't sometimes wish for control over other people or situations, and yet I can say that the length of time that it takes for me to let go and regain my balance has become dramatically shorter. The journey, that struggle to stay on the path, continues to this day. I am here to learn about love, letting go of who I think I am, joining the human race as one who belongs to everyone.

Because I have difficulty seeing myself from the inside, I want to share with you a note that the associate pastor of my church wrote to me following a sermon that I delivered on New Year's eve of 2006. The text is included in this book as an essay titled "The culture of recovery," on page 109. She wrote,

"I want you to know how grateful I am that you are in this world -- that you have developed the gifts of courage, empathy, compassion and embodying hope. I know the struggle to be where you are has been long and difficult, and all the more, the struggle has made you authentic, humble, and strong. What you offered of your story, of yourself to the congregation on Dec. 31 has impacted so many -- just last night, again, this powerful service came up in conversation in a meeting I was part of and I wanted you to know the depth and beauty of the conversation that followed. Here are a few of the things I heard:

'The courage David showed in being 'real' gives me courage and permission to be more real with others in our church.'

'I resonated with David's story, identified with so much he said. His is a story of profound transformation and I needed to hear it.'

'David was so confident and clear. I was so moved that he trusted his church family enough to share his powerful story.'

'This service will stay with me for a long time.'

I wanted you to know what I heard. It is so good to have you among us, David. what a blessing you are to this world and what a lesson for all to learn from, that there is hope for us to move from violence to a true and lasting peace -- that hope is alive and walking around in you, David." -- Melanie Oomen

In conclusion, it should be obvious that my descent into the damaging violence of addiction was a result of my fears. I made a choice to withdraw from, and distrust, interaction with the rest of humanity. I imagined myself to be a grand and unique victim of circumstances beyond my control.

My journey back to wholeness has been a collaborative effort on the part of hundreds of fellow "victim volunteers," quite a few therapists, sponsors, mentors, my supportive family members, and amazing circumstances beyond my control that I attribute to my Higher Power. Letting my old vanity evaporate, L.O.V.E., has been both my process and my goal.

I feel like a winner, the recipient of a marvelous gift beyond anything I could have achieved through my own struggle and effort. I feel blessed beyond any selfish desires I may have had for comfort and security.

Essays of encouragement

These essays were written as blog entries over approximately a five-year period. They generally reflect my goal of empowering others to find their response-ability.

Victim, rebel, or co-creator?

Our ability to recover from a culture of violence depends greatly upon our self-confidence that we have the resources to accomplish the task. If we believe we are a victim of the system, the power to change that system resides in the hands of other people. If we adopt the role of a rebel against the system, then all our anger and blame can be directed against it. Both victim and rebel are reactions to what appears to be a static situation. However, if we shift our thinking and believe we are co-creators of a dynamic system, we are free to take responsibility for our part in it. This initial change that begins within ourselves provides the inspirational energy, the hope, the idea, for others near us and the entire culture, to recover.

I find that when I attach expectations to my activism for peace, based on my notion of what it means to succeed, then my actions become a kind of co-dependency, an attempt to control, direct, or manipulate other people. How I feel and act becomes dependent on, and reactive towards, how well their actions fulfill my expectations. When I try to manipulate others I am part of the problem instead of being part of the solution. I lose my independent creativity and become easily discouraged, resentful, even cynical. I have found that for my activism to be sustainable, it has to be grounded in the dance and fearless spontaneity of love and in letting go of results.

In my role as a community organizer for a culture of peace, I am constantly challenged by

encounters with the victim attitude, in which people will communicate their feeling of powerlessness by saying *"I'm glad you're doing this work,"* which I translate to mean *"Change is good. You go first."* The implication is that I am somehow capable of making the change for them and that I have more power than they do. I have observed of myself and other peace-builders that we regularly buy into this illusion of grandiosity, that we are the only ones doing the really important work, that very few people seem to truly care or support what we are doing. We see ourselves as martyrs to the cause, an enormously impossible task which we will heroically endure anyway. We adopt the victim meme.

This is my judgement of the peace movement: it has been too goal-oriented, task-oriented, and doomed to feeling uniquely burdened with the mission of controlling the violence in the world. It becomes a struggle, and the struggle has pushed the goal away. Typically, peace activists see only a small part of the entire systemic problem because they only inventory the faults of the status quo. If there is no inventory of its strengths included as well, and if our personal faults and strengths are omitted, we create an "analysis paralysis." That leads to our feeling like a self-pitying victim.

I find myself having to back off, relax, go with the flow, and humble myself again and again. To attempt to break the door down, bust the barriers to recovery, is folly. The truth is that *humanity is a learning organism*, and thanks to modern communication technology, we are learning extremely rapidly in the context of long-term history. I am one 7-billionth of an entire organism that is dissolving and re-creating itself in unpredictable directions every day!

Yes, we feel the urgent threat of species extinction deep in our souls. Sixty-five million years ago, a mass extinction event was initiated when an asteroid hit the earth. Now another mass extinction event is in full swing at the rate of possibly 30,000 species every year,[52] and we are just beginning to see that humanity's effect on the planet is not much different than that of an asteroid.

In the middle of this ecosystem catastrophe, there is another kind of collapse, a collapse that may not necessarily be negative. Many people compare it to the dissolution of the caterpillar so that a butterfly can emerge. Our democracy is in a crisis. Those at the center of government seem to be unresponsive to the people. Many people wish for greater moral, legal, and intelligent behavior in our government. Our security is being threatened, and our economy is being drained of untold hundreds of billions of dollars by the direct and indirect consequences of violent conflict in our homes, our streets, our schools, and our prisons. The direct and indirect cost of US military involvement in violent conflict is currently $1.2 trillion annually.[53] This includes not only the Department of Defense but also defense-related spending in other departments, such as the nuclear weapons programs in the Department. of Energy. Who is to say that mankind, with enough nuclear bombs to destroy all life on the planet several times over, shall continue? The healthy growth and development of children and the prosperity of adults is at risk. The dream of a united humanity seems very distant.

This is it. Within our lifetime, our planet will be transformed, for better or worse, and we are ultimately the ones who are able to respond (be responsible). As individuals we did not cause this planetary disease, we can't control it, and we can't cure it. However, if each one of us is a potential mutation of the oppressor-victim meme, the virus of recovery can spread quickly over the entire body of humanity.

Imagine this news story: A benign (B-9) virus epidemic is causing massive outbreaks of peace. B-9 is very contagious, especially among young children and the elderly. The most common means of transmission are hugs in excess of 20 seconds in length, and peace symptoms are also suspected of coming from long walks on ocean beaches or in deep mountain forests. Individual symptoms include difficulty in dominating other people, willingness to listen for long periods without interrupting, and forgetting to lock the house, as well as spontaneous outbursts of joyful singing and tears of gratitude. An epidemic may be indicated by improved learning in schools, shortages of workers, empty jails, and closure of military recruiting offices. Government epidemiologists say control is impossible, since the B9 virus will disassemble the DNA of fear-based opinions with outbursts of laughter. The prognosis is for long-term chronic peace to dissolve religious, political and national boundaries, blend the races into one soft brown color, and marginalize the use of currency as a representation of value. The B9 virus is very dangerous to the status quo and should be treated with respect.

This may be very entertaining to contemplate, and we must also be very serious. Creating a non-violent world is not easy right now. We all want the security and prosperity of peace, and yet the personal inner work necessary to manifest the social outer peace is much more difficult than we ever anticipated. Why? Our culture has provided us with infinite varieties of denial, distraction, and delusion that all seem to be plausible alternatives to the ugly truth about ourselves and our complicit participation. We are re-programming an entire system with vast inertia that is both external and internal. We

[52] http://www.whole-systems.org/extinctions.html

[53] http://www.tomdispatch.com/archive/175361

must not be complacent about this. With all our care and attention we must hold our fingers on the "reset" button constantly to prevent the program of violence from re-invading our lives.

When the *Twelve Steps of Personal Peacemaking* are read for the first time, it's quite possible that they elicit a less-than-enthusiastic response. Denial and rationalization may dismiss them as unnecessary, trivial, somebody else's problem, or even impossible to implement. These reactions avoid the central question: do we personally choose to recover from our immersion in a culture of violence? Do we even see that we have been affected by the violence?

On the other hand, do we realistically have the option to maintain the status quo by absolving ourselves of any personal responsibility for changing it? The human species is facing extinction from our failure to implement our greatest strength, cooperation.

I used to be a violent-thinking person. I was victimized by domestic violence and school-yard bullying as a child. I was terrorized by the prospect of nuclear annihilation in the 1950's, and I became an angry, explosive, suicidal teenager. I saw that the cause of the violence I was receiving at the hands of my father was no different than the cause of the violence between nations: the inability to communicate. Violence is a form of non-verbal communication that says "Get away from me, I don't want to talk to you, I can't deal with the feelings." We know that skillful diplomacy and extended dialog can prevent the violence that we rationalize as "punishment."

I learned how to be non-violent by re-learning how to perceive and how to talk. I see things differently now. Now I have discovered that there are many millions of people just like myself, who care deeply about integrity, authenticity, respect for others and the future of humanity. America, and the rest of the world, is waking up. I am optimistic, because we, the people, are giving up being a tough John Wayne in order to be a generous Johnny Appleseed. The strength and power of America resides in the hearts and minds of its ordinary citizens, the people.

International security is patriotic

America's appearance as an imperial dominating force in the world has some severe problems associated with it. Through our technology we have led the world to the brink of total interconnectedness as well as to the brink of total annihilation. In doing so, we have painfully discovered that we have a greater responsibility than to just ourselves. We need to stand back as a nation and ask ourselves: Are we going toward a world that works for only a few, or a world that works for everyone? Is there some other way to adapt to the threats that we face? The time has come for us to reinvent ourselves. If we are to survive as a culture -- if we are to survive as a species -- we must use our real strength and real courage to relate to people instead of trying to dominate them.

"The weak come forward with a clenched fist – the strong with an open hand." --- William Kelly

We can continue to live in fear of violent conflict, war and terrorism, or we can courageously accept international disagreements as a call for deeper communication. It is natural to fear attack, conflict, anger, and disagreement. However, when we as a nation use defensive thoughts, words and deeds to build strong walls around ourselves because we believe the "best defense is a good offense," then we have put ourselves into the hell of solitary confinement, apart from the other nations. Now is the time to make a new choice.

Although we may have some success with constant preparedness for fighting, struggle, or mortal combat, and there certainly are times when we run out of options, I would suggest that there is a another way, and I hope it sounds a bit outrageous to you. We are no longer limited to life as victims of a system of win-lose, manipulation, separation, and exploitation of sex, money, and power. We have the power to take responsibility for our role in shaping the culture in which we live. We have the power of imagination, our greatest gift, with which we can and will subvert the domination system. Our struggle is no longer with an external "enemy." Our struggle is to imagine ourselves using our innate ability to communicate honestly and openly, to use our vulnerability to get our needs met, to transcend our fear of other people as a matter of national policy. This is our gift to the world and our gift to ourselves, our own personal recovery becoming a national and cultural recovery. This is the revolution which will turn the world upside down, for the better.

When a nation is addicted to hyper-vigilance and the use of offense as the best defense, peace is most often seen as unpatriotic, the antithesis of the national identity. In this context, peace is perceived as passive and defenseless, unlike the patriot who "vigorously supports their country (their *patris*, fatherland) and is prepared to defend it against enemies or detractors," as defined in the dictionary. The problem with the word "defense" is its conflation with "offense," power, domination, and isolation, which are currently the most common strategies to produce security. The Department of Defense was previously named the War Department.

The demonstrated powerlessness of the United States to dominate a small group of determined fighters, and the inability of the U.S. to isolate itself from the current mass extinction event is illuminating the underlying need for a long-lasting, sustainable security. Patriotism is really about security, and if we look more closely at what long-term sustainable security could look like, it starts to look like peace.

Patriotic peace means vigorous support for the economic, health, and relationship security of the land and people with whom we live. Thus, whatever strategy creates economic security is patriotic. Whatever creates health security is patriotic. If something diminishes threats by creating relationships of trust and cooperation, it's patriotic. A partnership-based dialog process that is neither passive nor defenseless, that creates expanding opportunities to satisfy every human need, is patriotic. The difficult, courageous work of creating peace through non-violent strategies then becomes a challenge for us to express our most honorable and virtuous character traits.

Cynics create prisons

The cynic is a great believer in individualism, and self-interest. They will tell you that corruption, power struggles, and wars are the inevitable result of human nature. They will say things like *"The military is there to protect the U.S. The world is not a nice place. It's filled with injustice, that's why we need a strong U.S. defense."*

These comments are the epitome of the viewpoint of the cult of the individual which isolates us from the rest of the world. It is essentially a suicidal view. If we expect and see only danger, and cultivate a bunker mentality of "us" against "them," then the military muscle, the fortifications within which we have put ourselves, not only keeps "them" out, it also keeps "us" in a relationship and socio-economic prison of our own making from which there is no escape. A mentality of extreme defensiveness creates a jail for its occupants. We are held inside walls of fear. We are enslaved to a war-making machine.

Force and the threat of force tend to hold a "problem" in place. Fighting, domination, and manipulation create a static situation in which we assume that the person who disagrees with us will not change and that becomes a self-fulfilling prophecy. Although victories may be won, they become part of an endlessly repeating cycle of renewed combat. This is a type of slavery.

Inevitably, we feel ourselves to be stuck in an unchangeable world, and therefore we become depressed and apathetic, a victim of our own unfulfilled expectations.

"We are not victims of the world we see; we are victims of the way we see the world."
— Dennis Kucinich

The cynic wants other people to change without changing themselves. I have had this attitude, myself. It is the perfect set-up for addictive behavior, repeating the same mistakes while expecting different results, and all the time feeling like a victim of circumstances beyond our ability to control. We who are very ill with our victim stance are unable to consider other possibilities for solving problems and conflicts. The only behavior we know is fight or flight. We have a deep, paranoid attitude about alternative conflict resolution methods. We deny the expensive and wasteful consequences of violence through false pride and bravado.

This allows the cycle of violence to continue. We create, enable and sanction violent criminals by housing them in institutions of violence education -- our prisons -- or paying assassins or dictators to enforce our political will in other countries. We ourselves become criminal by cheating the system, breaking laws in both small and large ways. We are not a free country. We have the largest percentage of our population in prison of any nation. We are all in a prison of our own making. Violent thoughts, words and deeds, coming from the desire to be right, build the walls of solitary confinement. Do we want to be right, or do we want to belong to the human race?

Nuclear weapons represent the extreme end of the sociopathic mentality in which the use of the weapon is "right" and the victim is "wrong," regardless of how self-destructive the use of the weapon might be. There is no limited, clean, contained, precision targeting of such a weapon. It is both genocidal and ecocidal, eventually suicidal. It is obvious now that mega-bombs deter nothing. We are more vulnerable to multiple forms of attack than ever before. Nuclear weapons became obsolete on the day they were first tested!

It's time to admit our violence is out of control, time heal our broken hearts and seek reconciliation. Do we respect ourselves enough to do this? Do we feel capable and worthy, as our Constitution says, of a *more perfect Union, [to] establish Justice, [and] insure domestic Tranquility?"* The quickest way to recover our self-respect is to act our way into a new way of thinking, to be the change we wish to see in the world. We cannot expect it to come from outside ourselves.

Games People Play: The Psychology of Human Relationships is a 1964 bestselling book by psychiatrist Eric Berne.[54] This book catalogs a series of "games" in which ordinary people converse in a patterned way which appears superficially plausible or normal. However, there are actually private, concealed motivations in the conversation, which lead to a well-defined, predictable, counterproductive outcome. One of those games that I distinctly recall is *"Ain't It Awful,"* and it reinforces our self-identification as victims.

[54] Berne, E, Games People Play, Grove Press, 1964

When I read a long list of complaints against the status quo, or I hear despair in conversation or written comments, I hear the beating of the drums of alarm and fear. If the arguments are brought to the ultimate conclusion of their logic, it leads to desperate and violent acts of defiance. I look for the hidden assumption, which is usually that whoever is making the argument has no power, or that there is no external force, person, or situation that will change the world to their definition of security, prosperity and quality of life. Therefore, there is no hope. In a sense, they want the opposite to be true, to be in control, top dog, righteous. Their indignation, anger, and anguish includes a belief that the best strategy for a better world is to exclude certain people, not include everybody. The boundary of that exclusion zone has to be forcefully defended for the world to be safe.

On the other hand, when we imagine ourselves being fearless in genuine relationships with other people, when we escape from the fantasies about how dangerous other people might be -- how they need to be controlled, dominated, or even eliminated -- there is no struggle, there is only surrender to a wonderful sense of belonging, trust, and safety. Is that not what we all really want, anyway?

Are we willing to try something different: creating power with others instead of over them, surrendering to the needs of the greater good instead of clinging to the egotistical needs of the individual?

I am saying it is better to be a generous rose than a tough, gun-slinging cowboy. It is better to create the conditions for the resolution of conflict through empathetic heart-to-heart communication, not the kind of talking-at-people-in-order-to-win that is the hallmark of people with low self-esteem.

Rebels seek magic

A few years ago I left the meeting of the Eugene Peace Coalition feeling weary, discouraged, confused, sad and distressed. How can such good-hearted people not see their own good hearts? The anti-war movement has always had the option of pulling off a magic trick, and has sadly held itself back from exercising its own power of imagining into existence the joy, wonder, and fulfillment of people working together in community.

On the way home, I heard on the radio *The Galaxy Song*[55] about being on this small green planet flying through space, and I thought about how when we are ready to fall asleep in our beds, we are in a moment of stability and security, unaware that we are racing through space at 40,000 miles per hour. We often don't see the big picture, the background of stars and galaxies in which we rest. Fortunately, this is not a problem for us. It seems natural, right, harmonious, secure.

On the other hand, when we in the anti-war movement focus on such issues as resisting the conspiring power of a shadow government, there is no harmony. We are in a moment of instability and insecurity. If we could see the background in which we lie sleepless with anxiety, we might have a different perspective on our struggle. Our insecurity is part of the problem.

War in all its forms, including war on Nature, continues and threatens to engulf the world in what might be the end of most life on this planet, even the lives of those who wage war. We are looking into the abyss with a great deal of understandable anxiety, bordering on terror and panic. This is the time when many people ask themselves, *"What the hell am I doing here?"*

---

[55] by Eric Idle of Monty Python

Indeed. What the hell are we doing? Why are we here and what is our goal? If we feel angry about war and violence, that feeling does not necessarily tell us what our goals are. If the activists in the anti-war movement are successful in stopping this war, even preventing the next one, is that the end of the anti-war movement? Or is there something beyond? Would a peace treaty simply mean a lull until the next war, or would it create a sustainable future, a future of cooperation and mutual respect? In the struggle to tear down the giant, the war-producing domination system, I think something has been overlooked: what do you imagine could replace domination. Suppose the wars ended tomorrow, suppose the whole rat pack of enabling politicians were removed from office, disgraced. Where would we be? What could be next? Would the domination system actually be gone? What about global corporations?

It gets to be a bit overwhelming, doesn't it? At the Peace Coalition I heard the voice of weariness clinging to shreds of hope, and I'm sure many others feel the same way. Wouldn't it be great if we had a miracle? Miracles are simply shifts in visible reality where the relationship of cause to effect is not apparent. The anti-war movement is already producing an unexpected event with an unseen cause. Could it be that when we expect to do battle with a powerful, dark and sinister adversary, we have unwittingly defined ourselves as victims and martyrs in the bargain? I am sure this particular miracle is not the one we wanted.

Our attitude, our position, our angle of attack, our definition of the problem determines the outcome. The anti-war movement remains oppositional in its strategies, and the opposition does not lose strength in this struggle. It becomes stronger. If you scream every day at teenagers not to have sex, use drugs, or get pierced, guess what they are going to run out and do. When classroom teachers believe in their students' potential, and then encourage and support high standards of performance from their students, guess what occurs. Expectations are powerful.

Without clearly defined goals, the movement tends to wander in multiple, angry directions. The fractured pieces of the anti-war movement seem to struggle for hegemony, criticize those who are unwilling to be arrested, hate those who think wars are necessary, fight for control and defeat of the shadow government, and yet somehow still expect something positive (is it peace and love?) to spring forth. But from where? From angst? Would someone please explain to me how being against something is a goal. I assert that working for the absence of something is not a goal at all, but a strategy for an undefined goal.

If we can agree on that kind of future as the one most desirable, then we can reasonably evaluate our strategic alternatives. The pro-warrior believes in peace through the strength of domination. The anti-warrior believes in strength through the peace of cooperation and understanding. Are they not both talking about the creation of stability and security, survival? The big picture is that both groups are on converging tracks toward the same goal whether they can see it or not. The desire for security and stability appears to be emerging among many people as a very clearly defined and overriding priority. When it becomes clear enough that we all want the same things in the end, we will see a quantum leap into solutions that work for everybody, including the people we may currently consider to be idiots. When the anti and pro-war activists are able to define and communicate their goals to each other as equals, war will cease to be a problem. Now that would be a miracle, wouldn't it?

Product designers will tell you that any problem is composed of four parts: an unrealized but clearly defined goal, barriers to the goal, resources for resolving the problem, and alternative courses of action. When *all* parts of the problem are completely defined, the solution appears. I want to say here "as if by magic," yet there is no magic to it when you understand the mechanism that remains hidden in the background.

We ignore background phenomena constantly. That is a natural part of being human. The anti-war movement seems to be unaware that a quantum leap is now in progress into fearless cooperation by millions of people worldwide. This leap is making that shadow government obsolete, ineffective, and powerless, at "40,000 miles per hour" (the speed of Earth's flight through space) to boot. We are, and always have been, individually and collectively, a self-healing, self-correcting organism in search of stability, just like every other organism on the planet and the planet herself. This is the unseen background to the attack on war. We are at war with ourselves, externally, brother against brother, and internally, mind against heart.

> *"Why didn't you fight back against the Chinese?"*
>
> *The Dalai Lama looked down, swung his feet just a bit, then looked back up at us and said with a gentle smile, "Well, war is obsolete, you know."*
>
> *Then, after a few moments, his face grave, he said, "Of course the mind can rationalize fighting back...but the heart, the heart would never understand. Then you would be divided in yourself, the heart and the mind, and the war would be inside you."*

We are at war with ourselves. We are deathly ill with interpersonal and systemic violence inflicted on ourselves. Our vain attempts to be secure have left us exhausted, empty of resources, and questioning. The time is ripe for genuine weeping, empathy for ourselves and others, and a radical shift in our strategies for achieving security, health, and growth. Rugged individualism has lost its virtue. Compassionate community is the more believable, trustworthy focus of our efforts. This is easy to say, yet hard to implement -- today. Just give it a few more days.

What is sane leadership?

Resilient people are creating an alternative to the domination system, and they are triggering others to imagine themselves in action. Given the difficulty that most people have in making decisions about what actions to take, I am guessing that the pressure to make good decisions is only going to increase, and the importance of leadership that models *sanity* will become acute. My hope is that our communication technologies will be able to rapidly disseminate sane decision-making models when the stress reaches its peak. I hope there will be the opportunity for the introduction of peace-building practices that actually work. My belief is that much of the necessary peace-building knowledge is already embedded in the non-governmental culture, waiting for just such an opportunity.

What truly gives us the power to change the world is our own attitudes. The people who abolished slavery and the people who gave women the right to vote refused to be overwhelmed, refused to be victims of "the system." The systemic institutions of violence can be dismantled. It may be a long and arduous path, and if we the people give up before we even get started, we actually support the continuation of that violence, we are complicit with it. How can we give ourselves permission to be who we truly are, to be aware of our mission in life, and to have a wonderful adventure while doing it? We can learn to have detached playfulness, creativity and resilience. These are the characteristics of someone who can navigate through difficulties to a better world.

Al Siebert has listed these qualities of a highly resilient person: [56]

- Playful, childlike curiosity
- Constantly learning from experience
- Adapts quickly
- Has solid self-esteem and self-confidence
- Has good friendships, loving relationships
- Expresses feelings honestly
- Expects things to work out well
- Reads others with empathy
- Uses intuition, creative hunches
- Defends self well
- Has a talent for serendipity
- Gets better and better every decade

As we become more resilient -- stronger, more resourceful, more imaginative, more creative, and more response-able -- that strength becomes contagious, and we become leaders. The power of collaboration and community can be better elicited by people who do not spread fear but instead inspire hope by their actions.

I have become convinced that I have the power to mid-wife this world into one that is free of domination. I believe that all it takes to birth this world is for me to transform myself into a more mature, responsible, and loving person. That's all I have to do, nothing more than that, nothing less than that. Nothing is more important than that transformation. When I change my inner world, my external behavior shifts to match, and I become a creative source of systemic change.

Moreover, if I can do it, with my history of dysfunction and wounding, certainly you can do it. The ripple effect from this transformation is immeasurable, and it has the power to stimulate the largest institutions of repressive domination to implode. This turns conventional thought on its head, and would appear to be insane to most people, a kind of megalomania, which it is not. It is the exact opposite of megalomania. It is acknowledging our critical participation in energetic systems far larger than ourselves. It is saying we are co-creators.

I do not accept that I am the victim of the military-media-corporate-government conspiracy. I am 100% responsible to it, another apparently "insane" idea. What I mean is that I am 100% able to *respond* to it. I have an answer, a better alternative. I have the ability to generate more than one answer. Having a better idea is far more effective for producing social transformation than recrimination and revolt. Very soon the world will be ready to hear millions of people who have transformed themselves internally to be the change, and not demand the change from some external source.

I refuse to characterize myself as a victim of capitalism, globalism, or any *ism*. When I see myself as a victim, I define power as scarce, limited, in short supply, and belonging to someone or something else other than me. I have none, or very little power by comparison, and I need to "get some" as if it were "out there." This kind of thinking posits that health care, or full employment, or peace, is an object, a possession, a destination that can be purchased with power. This kind of thinking perpetuates the domination system, and confirms that the domination system exists within me, because I own it. I am responding to it exactly as those who dominate wish that I would respond to it, submissively, as someone whose power has been

---

[56] Seibert, Al, Ph.D., The Survivor Personality, Perigee Books/Berkley Publishing Group, 2010

stolen, or reactively, as someone without power trying to grab it.

I do not submit. I have the power to create an entirely different social structure. I have the power to create a world that works for all. It does not depend upon the domination system to disappear for me to engage in this creative act. If I persist in exercising my creativity I am absolutely certain that the domination system shall eventually collapse, implode, and die because it will be seen clearly as dysfunctional. This time, there will be no blood. The military-industrial complex will simply dry up and blow away, useless and unwanted.

No struggle, no rebellion, no acts of violence are necessary to destroy the domination system. The dominators are already in trouble and worried about their own survival, and they would be greatly reassured of their power if someone would only rise up in rebellion against it. How reassured will they be when we simply walk away from the battlefield? The presence of millions of culturally creative evolutionaries[57] everywhere on the planet is the beginning of that walk, and is now unstoppable.

The Occupy Wall Street movement is not a political movement, it is a movement of values. It is not a struggle for victory over, or modification of, the status quo. Such goals are short-sighted. There is no economic, political or technological change that will produce lasting benefit for our grandchildren unless it is accompanied by a dramatic shift toward the value of distributive justice -- a fair share of security, prosperity, and quality of life for all. It may look like a protest, but it is an abandonment of the culture of retributive justice (wealth, power, fear, survival of the fittest, win-lose, and exploitation of nature and one another). It is a public demonstration of the community we want to live in. It is an expression of an entirely new

and permanent culture of radical civic engagement, cooperative learning and problem-solving by consensus.

There is a rebirth in progress. The house of rigid, hierarchical, authoritarian, institutional structures is being replaced by flexible, horizontal, nurturing, familial networks. We are finally learning how to communicate, as in "commune," to build community. New technologies for communication are now affordable to billions of us. The Arab Spring is one outcome of that technology. The absolute best way for the activist community to move things forward to a sustainable future is to invent it in the present, to build it now, to do an end-run around the opposition. Allow the opposition to fall on its face, which it is doing rather rapidly.

Living in a militaristic society is like living in an alcoholic family. The bank account is drained to pay for the intoxicating power of weaponry and soldiers, everyone feels endangered, the significant other (the government) doesn't give a damn about your pain and suffering, and the addictive behavior ricochets off everyone, generation after generation.

The good news is that we can choose to be free of militarism. We have the power to let go with love and take care of ourselves. Allow the war-mongers, the nation-states and the corporations that support them to hit bottom, however that may happen. They are already close to bankruptcy, physically, morally, and spiritually. They do not have to take us with them into that dark place. We can allow them to experience the full consequences and reality of their behavior, a citizenry that no longer recognizes their legitimacy.

...by not tolerating and refusing to be a part of the old reality, as

---

[57] Ray, P. & Anderson, S. The Cultural Creatives: How 50 Million People Are Changing the World, Harmony, 2000

we literally cannot stomach it anymore, it makes us literally refuse to participate, therefore withdrawing any energy of support. If we do not become involved in something and negate it, it cannot survive because there is no energy to make it real and alive. It will simply cease to be as it will not be residing in anyone's consciousness. -- Karen Bishop

We can "move out" like one who leaves the home of an addict. We can re-create our lives, re-build patterns of behavior that support a sane and healthy future for ourselves and our children. We begin by examining how we have become complicit with militarism. We look at militarism as the tragic expression of an unmet need, and then create alternative strategies for human security. There are many success stories to choose from, and millions of people world-wide have formed support networks for this transition.

The response-ability is ours, at the grassroots, to invent and create the joy, wonder and power of people working together -- co-creating -- in harmonious community. This is the real revolution, this is the revolution that needs no funds, no power, no television coverage. We can overcome the obstacles of privilege and power to create an evolutionary, inclusive culture at the fringes of humanity, where all true survival strategies originate, such as where the marginalized peoples live. They have supportive social networks that are exemplary models for living in the midst of "crisis."

World peace will arrive when we feel that we belong to all people, they belong to us and when we are certain that we will never be abandoned. That feeling is a source of power. When we explore what is within then what is without will, as if by a miracle, seem smaller and less powerful. We become the hero we have been waiting for. It seems that nothing is more beautiful than we are. Nothing. We have all the resources within us that we need. We get to choose. We get to undo the choices we have made in the past. We create our future. We always have, even when we didn't see *how* we were creating our future. We always will decide what our abilities are for response. We can fly, and we know where we are going.

Letting it all hang out, warts and all, being fully honest about ourselves, that's where we are going. When we are so comfortable with ourselves that we have no enemies, then no-one can hurt us, and we no longer struggle. We laugh, love, and live in peace.

I invite you to invest in peace, to take a risk, to stretch yourself, to start small if you need to, and add more later. Ask yourself, would an investment of time, energy or money make me feel more wealthy or less wealthy in my sense of partnership and collaboration, the root cause of peace? If not now, when? If not me, then who?

One person can change the world. My friend Liz Graydon teaches middles school in New York City, and uses the 1982 movie *"Gandhi"* in her curriculum. She says her students are invariably skeptical that nonviolence could accomplish anything. One boy conceded that the film was pretty convincing and then added, "But c'mon, Miss Graydon, there are 6 billion people on the planet. You'll never get all of them to be nonviolent."

She pointed out that the population of India when it became liberated by Gandhi's movement was 300 million. So if one Gandhi can liberate 300 million, then "We don't need 6 billion Gandhis," she told him. "We need 20 Gandhis."[58]

---

[58] Koehler, R., Twenty Gandhis, Tribune Media Services, August 31, 2006

On Sept. 7, 2001, the United Nations passed a resolution to make Sept. 21 the International Day of Peace. This was the outcome of one person living his values: Jeremy Gilley.

He campaigned tirelessly for four years with students and peace activists, presidents, dignitaries and leaders around the world to make the International Day of Peace a fixed, memorable day instead of the variable, forgettable day previously established in 1981.

As a result, the International Day of Peace is now celebrated by people all over the world, and is expanding its reach every year. We may not hear about it, but there are proclamations, ringing of bells, prayers and meditations, concerts and festivals, and many people take a moment of silence at noon. This day brings forth the longing for not only peace but also for the prosperity and security that follows peace and supports an upward spiral of peace. I believe the more conscious we are of our subtle and deeply held values, the more our behavior becomes congruent with those values. I think this kind of integrity is what sustained Jeremy on the long journey to his goal.[59] His expression of his longing for peace inspires us. Now it is our turn. Peace can be contagious.

The wave of transformation is happening all around us if we are open to perceiving it, and it is time to paddle like hell to match our speed with the wave so that when it breaks we are surfing forward and not left behind. Those who ascribe to the *"Left Behind"* series of fictions, those who cling to blaming others and feeling superior, who refuse to accept that we are all in this together, are in for a big surprise.

For us to achieve world stability and security, otherwise known as "peace," we must decide to give up fighting for control, struggling for hegemony, or opposing everyone who is not in agreement with us as well-meaning zealots are prone to do. We must become a global stabilizing influence. On the face of it, our culture will tell us this is not a "rational" course of action because it doesn't fit with the familiar, short-term goals of win-lose. Yet deeper examination of long-term goals (i.e., what is good for the seventh generation?) reveals that the strategy of win-win and cooperation makes the most sense. Do we really have any choice? The winner in a win-lose paradigm automatically becomes a victim of their own self-isolation. A desire for revenge is likely to arise, and they have lost the joy, wonder, and power of people working together in community.

Most people will tell you that they would prefer to live in the non-violent, peaceful, and beloved community that Martin Luther King Jr. and Gandhi envisioned. Yet they are in despair about our culture ever providing that for them. As soon as the dilemma is reframed as our personal need to uncover -- release -- our ability to respond to our frustration, our anger, our sadness, with creative solutions, that problem disappears. It becomes easy to build supportive community and expand it.

From my own experience in the struggles of recovery, and from what I have heard in the stories of other people, the toxic shame and guilt that we carry seems to be the greatest stumbling block to not only accepting ourselves as we are, both good and bad, but also accepting that we are accepted.

> *"You are accepted!" . . . accepted by that which is greater than you and the name of which you do not know. Do not ask the name now, perhaps you will know it later. Do not try to do anything, perhaps later you will do much. Do not seek for anything, do not*

---

perform anything, do not intend anything. Simply accept the fact you are accepted." — Paul Tillich

It seems to me that once I have let go of my self-humiliation, which is simply the flip side of arrogance -- feeling unique and therefore separate -- I can be truly humble and accept the present situation, no matter how bad it may seem, and what it is bestowing upon me. I can open my mind to the possibility of different and new, often extremely surprising, outcomes -- ones that don't necessarily meet my demands. I am ready for outcomes that I never could have planned with my limited knowledge. I begin to relax my struggle against the status quo. I become a participant in the change, the evolution.

We all want to arrive, quite naturally, quickly and safely on the other shore of what has been described as a paradigm shift, a great turning of civilization. However, there is the matter of the frightening, chaotic, unknown place -- the lake, the abyss, the void, which must be crossed. You could say our culture is dying. Just as individuals die, leaving this shore to make a transition to another life, there comes a moment when all certainty of what we thought we knew, is swept away. Nothing works any more, no effort avails us, unexpected things happen, chaos is unleashed. Fear can grip our hearts when we become angry, rigid and obsessed, attempting the same efforts over and over. If the chaos extends more than a few hours or days, we can become depressed or apathetic, even suicidal or homicidal.

There is a panic-driven homicide on a global scale happening now. Humanity's suffering is difficult to look at, and other species are faring even worse. We are all in the midst of a catastrophe, in a mass extinction event that is in full swing already -- there is no turning back. The abyss yawns in our path. We catch glimpses of the extinction of other species, and we begin to wonder, could we be next? The thought is very sobering. I cannot bear for more than a few minutes to contemplate the full extent of the damage, nor the uncertainty about how long it will continue.

We cannot know how long it will take until we have true world peace. From my own experience, when things are looking dark and impossible, the most empowering thing that I can do for myself is to give up the result I want and become fascinated with the process instead.

Social evolution does not occur gradually as a result of a dialectical opposition and conflict between "the movement" and "machiavellian forces," but through an attraction to higher levels of functioning. How discouraging, how depressing it would be if we were engaged in endless contests of strength! As the diagram by Ervin Laszlo on page 20 would suggest, change occurs in sudden revolutionary jumps with a rapid influx of attractive, new information in response to a survival threat. I believe Buckminster Fuller showed great insight when he said,

> *"You never change anything by fighting the existing. To change something, build a new model and make the existing obsolete!"*

The new model of social process now evolving will make sense to both ends of the political spectrum and everyone in between. It will be a win-win. It will not be a process of reform followed by push-back. Polarization will dissolve.

For me, change is inevitable and evolutionary, and I can be an agent of change by remaining in the attractive energy. When I am utterly convinced there is another shore, and we are moving toward it, carried by winds that we cannot see, that vision strengthens others' willingness to raise their sails. When I indulge in self-pity, regrets, blame, or anger, I am tearing my own sails. Of course, I do that quite regularly! That's why I had to write this book.

This paradigm shift, this crisis, this revolution is our opportunity to practice empathy with ourselves and others. We become stronger, more resourceful, more response-able when we practice empathy. That strength moves by attraction from the strong to the weak. The old-timers need the newcomer to keep the empathy flowing, to get outside of themselves, to let the world collapse and go with it, to bow to their utter powerlessness. In the giving of empathy, we discover the essence of non-violence -- the irrational truth of our own inner spirit that cannot be damaged or lost -- and our equality with each other. A terrific book that explores this entire issue is *"When Love Meets Fear"* by David Richo.[60]

The peacemakers are in recovery from living in a domination paradigm, and every one of them is a leader. A leader is simply someone who owns the desired result by saying to him or herself, *"this is my destiny, to be free from violence, this is mine to do."* So it could be anyone. It can be you.

Perhaps self-respect is the bottom line. Perhaps when we feel like broken victims our righteous outrage numbs out, chokes up, stalls. How many people actively think that our destiny is an end to violence or that it is natural for humans to live in peace? I think it's very real in our culture that many of us -- most of us -- unconsciously judge ourselves as not ready for world peace, having little value in the effort to get there. As we think of ourselves, so we think of others. The real work of the activists for peace is to be so accepting and appreciative of themselves that their self-respect becomes the basis for claiming peace for themselves and others.

I had an epiphany about leadership on Martin Luther King day a few years ago. I was out walking in the morning, thinking about Martin, wishing he were still alive, wishing someone would fill his shoes. I heard geese honking, and I looked up from my shaded spot to see a formation of geese brilliantly lit by the morning sun, so bright that they seemed to be like angels. I wasn't sure they were Canada geese. I remembered how all the honking is encouragement to the leader, who serves the flock by breaking the wind and creating lift for the goose that follows, how that lift gets passed along from bird to bird, and how the leader rmoves to the back when it gets tired. Let's get honking!

Martin was a lead goose. Gandhi was a lead goose. They have rotated to the back. Now it's our turn to create their dream of the beloved community.

> *"If we have as much sense as a goose, we will stay in formation with those who are headed the same way we are. People who share a common direction and sense of community can get where they are going more easily because they are traveling on the thrust of one another.*
>
> *"When the lead goose in formation gets tired, it rotates back in the V and another goose flies the point. We should each take on the extra work of leading in our turn to benefit the group.*
>
> *"Geese honk from behind to encourage those up front to keep up their speed. They aren't yelling at them - they are*

---

[60] Richo, D., *When Love Meets Fear*, Paulist Press 1997.

encouraging them and trying to help them along because they know they will soon be in that position.

"If we have the sense of a goose, we will support each other, encourage each other, and lead in our turn."

-- Dr. Harry Clarke Noyes

All the darkness in the world cannot snuff out the light of one tiny candle. If you believe that a human being is like a beacon bonfire linked to other bonfires, then you can accept what Lynne McTaggart has said,

"You have far more power than you realize to heal yourselves, your loved ones, your communities, the planet."

Vision drives action

The possibility of world peace is often discounted as not only impractical, but counter to everything that has been taught to us from our childhood. World peace is unknown. We fear the unknown more than anything else. Solutions are unbelievable when they have not been adequately described. Seeing is believing, for most people, or at least very motivating. Ninety-eight percent of the world wants to see the blueprint, the map, the model, the movie. We have the communication tools to offer this.

Before Columbus set sail for the New World, he had to believe there was a land mass on the other side of the Atlantic Ocean. He thought it was Asia. Before we sent a man to the moon, someone had to believe it was possible. Before slavery was abolished, before women got the vote, very few people thought those

sweeping changes were possible. Some did and they didn't give up on their vision.

Someone had to imagine not necessarily how it could be done, just imagine that it was possible. Our greatest obstacle to world peace is in our own minds. When we believe it is possible, we imagine the goal. We set our feet on the path, and we set the possibility in motion. Taking one step at a time, we arrive at our destination.

Great accomplishments are always preceded by great vision. Now is the time to offer a vision based on what has already been created: practical solutions and methodologies for accepting diversity and ending domination violence between people. Imagine the end of violence between humans and other species, and violence done to the planet. Imagine a vision of a positive future -- a vision so concrete, so detailed, so validated, tested and proven, so economically beneficial -- that at least 20% of the world would buy it and take us past the "tipping point." Another 78% would soon see the advantages. The last, pathological 2% would still need some policing.

The establishment of the Environmental Protection Agency by Richard Nixon did not begin our commitment to the environment, yet it raised it to a much higher level of national priority, and so should it be with the interests of peace. Violent, interpersonal conflict and wars could become a quaint, although tragic, historical fact. What if the Pentagon could become like the Maytag repair man, with nothing to do and a budget the size of the current Department of Education? Think what great schools and universities we could create with a budget the size of the current Department of Defense!

The legislation promoted by The Peace Alliance that would create a cabinet-level Department of Peace is one such vision, and it is only one. The Quakers have a plan called "The Peaceful Prevention of Deadly Conflict." The

Mennonites have proposed "3D Security." The Physicians for Social Responsibility have legislation in the House for "SMART Security." You can envision another pathway if you like. Just make it specific, detailed with living examples.

These proposals overlap and echo each other. They represent what a dedicated community of visionaries can provide. There are many small communities like them that are beginning to interconnect and grow in strength and numbers. The wave is coming, the wave of revolutionary change in how we interact with the world.

The economic benefits of violence reduction are extremely attractive right now. The "peace dividend" of an economy based on building an awareness of nonviolent conflict resolution would be in the trillions of dollars, many multiples of what we are wasting on attempts to suppress and control violence.

In the last 40 years we have developed new technologies of cooperation that are based on the deep recognition of the equality of the needs of all human beings. Experiments in social change have been conducted, data has been collected, and the results are in. As a creative and intelligent people, the American people are now able to be as effective in addressing the sources of violence as in reacting to its symptoms. *This* is the new adventure in democracy! A silent, nonviolent, and underground revolution is in progress in America.

Americans have been infused with a willingness to explore and grow, an adventurous spirit that dates to well before the time of the Revolution of 1776.

"What do we mean by revolution? The war? That was no part of the revolution; it was only an effect and consequence of it. The revolution was in the minds of the people, and this was

effected from 1760 to 1775, in the course of fifteen years, before a drop of blood was shed at Lexington."
-- John Adams, writing to Thomas Jefferson

How adventurous are you? I am asking you to investigate and come to your own conclusions. We don't get hard answers unless we ask the hard questions. What are the root causes of violence? Is it a moral problem? Is it a public health problem? What is nonviolence, really, and how is it useful for resolving conflict? Who has used nonviolence, and how effective is it?

Who will bring moral, legal, and intelligent behavior to those at the center of the government? Who?

Who will bring restorative justice, reconciliation of enemies, peaceful conflict resolution, and true security to our world?

Who will bring healthy growth and development for children? Who will bring the prosperity that results from cooperative learning and problem-solving?

Who will bring the strength of a united, inclusive, beloved community out of a diverse humanity?

We, the people!

You can become involved in creating a change for the better.

Pick up the phone, talk to the staff of your members of congress, send a postcard. They know they live in a bubble of corporate lobbyists. They really do want to hear from you!

"The current crisis in our democracy has less to do with Congressional failure to express the will of the people and more to do with failure of people to express their will in a meaningful way."
-- Representative John Conyers

Join the movement, any movement, the one that harmonizes with your passion. Donate money, donate time, donate your talents. As Gandhi said, *"Whatever you do will seem insignificant, but it is very important that you do it."* Many small efforts, many small ripples of change, will create a tidal wave of change. Speaking of change, the other kind that jingles in your pocket, no successful movement went forward without the energy of money to solidly support it, so be loose with your change while you're making change. Volunteer organizers need phones, office equipment, heated spaces, etc.

Get the attention of the media. Express yourself in writing or however it feels best for you do it. Try carrying a colorful banner in a parade! Create public exposure to the idea of a peaceful and prosperous future. Hope and optimism are just as contagious as gloom and doom, so keep it upbeat.

We, the people, are waking up. The time has come to stretch, move, and play a part in creating a better world for ourselves and those who will come later.

Love -- your love -- will always win.

Love is the key we must turn
Truth is the flame we must burn
Freedom is the lesson we must learn
Love is what we came here for
Love is the opening door
No one could offer you more
    -- Lani Hall, "Love Song"

A Bridge to Peace

A friend of mine asked for some brief ideas on "Where do we go from here?" The person standing for peace knows where to go intuitively. What makes it real for them is the vision, the map, of the intermediate steps. One of the best ways to see the path forward is to start from the distant goal and ask what has to happen before that, and before that, etc. This is what I did. I started from the top goal and worked backwards to the more immediate goal to brainstorm these ideas for a bridge to world security.

Some day in the near future, within our lifetime: The U.S. Congress authorizes and funds a Department of Peace or something like it, perhaps transforming the Homeland Security, Education, Health and State Departments to be well-funded agencies focused on violence prevention and human development. Other departments in the government, even Congressmen, begin to catch on to the partnership model, and cooperation begins to replace competition within the government. Our foreign policy transforms into a renewed emphasis on development and diplomacy initiatives. The United Nations finally begins to realize its full potential to create healing and reconciliation among the nations, as they all cooperate to end starvation, water shortages, illiteracy, poverty, homelessness, and disease. The United Nations acquires greater loyalty from its members and their investing $60 billion per year provides shelter, health care, AIDS control, adequate nutrition for everyone on the planet over a 10-year period. Literacy and citizenship become universal. With healthy growth and development of children, and full employment of adults, the root causes of violence shrink to minor concerns, and cooperative problem-solving becomes the norm. The entire world experiences a renaissance of creative genius and wisdom. Instead of an individual being in competition with everyone, the whole world will be in support of each individual. Religions are no longer a source of violence created by obsolete dogma. Churches are de-institutionalized and spirituality is commonly integrated into everyday life.

Before that happens: We see definite signs of a culture recovering from violence. The pro-warriors agree that security is the goal. Lobbying develops into a highly creative art form. Eventually, enough members of Congress are getting so many postcards and phone calls from their constituents that they hold hearings, haggle over the details, and pass a bill into law that moves the original intent of a Department of Peace forward. The nation and the world are electrified by the idea of preventing wars and interpersonal violence, and other nations form similar Departments. After the first year of operation, statistical reports will show that prevention efforts have already saved hundreds of thousands of lives, increased productivity, and boosted the economy. The Nonviolent Peace-force mediators will be making headlines in the news. Nonviolence becomes a household word, and major conflicts transformed nonviolently are more common, recognized, and extolled. Corporations begin producing peace-building products and services on a large scale because people want them and it becomes profitable. The UN reforms into a more democratic, horizontal partnership of nations or local regional governments. Religious leadership is shared with lay persons, experiential testimony takes precedence over dogmatic beliefs, and ancient scripture is deeply understood.

Before that happens: The anti-warriors, the pro-peace-builders, and environmentalists agree that the means are the ends in the making. Networks of networks are formed for nationally coordinated conferences, education, and actions. They create a united movement that presents an in-depth evaluation of strategies for security on a cost-benefit basis. The movement takes ownership of media broadcast networks and produces nonviolent entertainment. The media provide news of progress in the environmental and nonviolence fields. There are educational programs on lifestyle change and citizenship skill-building. The level of inspiration and enthusiasm builds, more citizens walk the halls of Congress, door-belling for the end of violence. The Congressional aides respect their constituents, a few are enthusiastic supporters, and some ask challenging questions. Major funding is acquired from progressive globalized corporations who leverage their influence on U.S. Congress and the United Nations.

Before that happens: Many people learn how to be active in conflict resolution and show up in public wearing a Peace button, informing others about their hopes and dreams and enlisting their support. Small groups are meeting in kitchens regularly to learn about peace-building. They are receiving unexpected invitations to speak to even more groups. They organize public events and fundraisers, get noticed by radio and TV, walk in community parades. They have an e-mail list. Letters to the editor are published. They get to know the local violence-prevention agencies, city council members and other influential people in their community. They meet their Senators and Representatives in their local offices or town hall meetings. Sometimes their children come with them.

The Peace Alliance (promoting a U.S. Dept. of Peace) unites with just *one* other group, possibly Beyond War or the Nonviolent Peaceforce, as a first step toward the building of a much larger alliance. Partnership becomes the new trend among environmental, anti-war, and peace groups. Corporate partners are enlisted in support of economic sustainability. (This is already widespread!) Effective boycotts of corporations involved in damaging practices are organized. Specific plans are developed for re-tooling the weapons, petroleum and automotive industries into ultra-efficient organic production systems for new forms of transportation, housing, water purification, energy generation, agriculture.

A year from now: All the pro-peace groups who are working to build a culture of peace -- everyone from the social justice and environmental movements, and anyone else who wants to come -- meet in a large, open field. There are world-wide video linkups with similar audiences. Small donations from millions of people come pouring in. Some music, some meditation, and much conversation about goals occurs. Not much is said about strategies and no final conclusions are reached on the rational-intellectual level, but enough emotional-spiritual electricity is generated to fry the circuits of NBC and ABC. Fox News is speechless.

The culture of recovery

In the depths of winter, I finally learned that within me lay an invincible summer.

--- Albert Camus

I believe war will soon be viewed as obsolete. The atomic bomb became the next most obvious step when the knowledge and technique for its construction and use became available. Conflict resolution by nonviolent methods will also be seen as the next most obvious step since the knowledge and technique for doing so are now available. In the last 40 years, the science of communication and conflict resolution has been tested and validated. Peace-building courses of study are now available in over 450 colleges and universities. Countless non-governmental organizations are developing field-proven techniques for reducing violence in families, schools, gangs, prisons, and ethnic groups.[61] These efforts now need the funding and coordination of a national mission to develop these skills throughout America, top to bottom, side to side. Then, maybe just then, we can start feeling good about ourselves again.

Today, conflict resolution without violence has been researched, tested and designed. We can see a detailed vision of steps towards peace. Each step follows a logical sequence. The visions of war and violence as a solution to disagreement have begun to lose their validity, but the prototype structure for peace has yet to be replicated across our culture. It is like building a birdhouse. When the space is ready, the dove of peace arrives.

This is the mechanism of a what appears to be a miracle. Einstein said "imagination is more important than knowledge," because knowledge often falsely limits our field of possibilities. Facts come in the guise of being right, true and correct. They seem more solid than a reality that goes beyond what exists now. What America and the world needs right now is a loving, loyal seeing-eye dog with the imagination to lead us into a positive future.

I submit that building a culture, an infrastructure, of peace is a concrete, specific, and achievable goal of the anti-war/pro-peace movement. If the movement were to focus upon it, it would happen quickly because it would accelerate what is inevitable and in harmony with the other changes occurring on the planet. It would seem to be magical. We would all sleep better at night.

If you are skeptical or despairing about world peace, I wrote this for you. I also wrote this for myself, because in May of 2005 I was struggling with how to respond to the cynicism I was encountering in the people around me, the very same cynicism that I had experienced within myself only a few months before. I asked myself, "How did I get here?" One sleepless night, the words poured out of me in a torrent, and I spent the next several weeks trying to make coherent sense out of what I had written. Now, I speak from my heart to your heart, for the children of the world.

When I would say "Peace is inevitable" in order to provoke people into thinking something other than war being inevitable, I was very alarmed to discover that for many people the first gut-response to my statement was "Yeah, we all die." That is a kind of peace, but not what I had in mind! Then I would soften my statement with "eventually, maybe not in my lifetime." However, that allows for the possibility of another 60 years of incredibly destructive war, and I just cannot accept that.

I am convinced that peace is coming for several reasons, stated briefly here, and followed with longer explanations.

---

[61] Hawken, P., Blessed Unrest, Viking Press, 2007

1. Emerging world crises are pressing us to change our problem-solving methods.
2. Recent trends, largely unnoticed, lay the groundwork for a radical leap in humanity's ability to cooperate.
3. Societal change follows acceptance of individual responsibility. We are not victims of the system, we ARE the system.
4. I have been, and am being, transformed into a peaceful person by working to "fake it 'til I make it." If I can do it, you can too. It's fun!

Old solutions won't fix multiple crises

Paul Ray, in his on-line booklet, *The New Political Compass*, says

> *"It is easily arguable that our inept and corrupt politics is about to harm us. The West is about to face a cascade of crises that political business as usual cannot handle, whether it is led from the right or the left."* [62]

The cascading crises of global warming, peak oil and suicidal terrorism are making it obvious that we are all on one lifeboat together. In the midst of this crisis, we cast about for pieces of flotation. There are many options within reach when we look beneath the surface chaos.

The media is focused on the drama and fear of the most obvious power struggles. However, beneath the surface, the evolution of humanity does not look like a power struggle. It has no single leader, and it's occurring in small group conversations. The ship of fear and control is slowly being abandoned. We are about to witness a cultural leap into fearlessness, and the old media will soon lose their influence. The

cultures who can survive the current cascade of crises will be the ones who develop the skills of cooperation, trust, and absolute fearlessness.

How we think about and frame what we are doing is so much more important than what we are doing. The issue before us is not personal survival, it is *how we think* about our survival, our strategies of survival, and the real meaning of our survival. Global warming is not just inconvenient weather patterns, it's a mass extinction event, and our interdependence with all life forms on earth has marked *Homo sapiens* as an endangered species.

When the bees go extinct, they take an entire food chain with them. When the algae in the ocean die off, so does the food chain that depends on it. If we cut down a forest, runoff creates floods. The air and water become toxic. We are also highly interdependent with all cultures, all races, and all nations. For example, if we close the border to immigrants, fruit and vegetables rot in the fields or go up in price or disappear altogether. We can no longer use the strategy of killing each other to grab energy resources, because the outcome of warfare is a net loss of resources.

We open a vision of new possibilities when we reframe global warming or peak oil as our opportunity to cooperate in expanding our access to sustainable energy resources that have been until now unavailable to us at a price we can pay. And so it is with building the peace. Terrorism is reminding us to access communication skills that have been previously unused. Real strength, real self-esteem, comes from relating to people instead of dominating them. This is the core idea behind the thousands of citizen activists that are hammering away at building a new lifeboat of peace for all people. This boat is one of those possibilities, and my personal favorite, that arise from looking

---

[62] http://www.grassrootsforamerica.us/fertilizer/New-Political-Compass-Intro.shtml

beneath the chaos on the surface and reframing what we are doing on this planet.

Sarah van Gelder, in her YES! magazine article *Why the Next 10 Years Will Be Nothing Like the Last 10 Years* lists some of the major crises that are creating the pressure to find new solutions and new ways of finding solutions. They include climate change, antibiotic-resistant infections, declining supplies of oil, nuclear proliferation, unilateral foreign policies and the widening gulf between rich and poor. Traditional problem-solving methods have failed to have an impact on these issues. On the other hand, Gelder says "ecologists tell us that the fringes are the most productive parts of ecosystems, and innovations from the fringes of society are today seeding a future that can sustain us all." [63]

As an example, Van Gelder points to the city of Los Angeles which, with its first Latino mayor, has responded to air, water, and soil pollution with new initiatives to plant trees, create habitat and wetlands, and to reuse storm water for irrigation.

When we define ourselves as independent agents competing for mastery over a finite set of circumstances, we imply that we are surrounded by enemies in a hopeless situation. This can lead to homicide and, more often than that, to suicide. When we humbly see our place in the context of the larger system of humanity, we are much more likely to participate in solving complex problems which may have otherwise seemed overwhelming. The willingness to cooperate is the new touchstone of sanity. It leads to not just survival, but an abundantly joyous survival.

When we act as if we are in unity and solidarity we learn how to make unity and solidarity real. The greatest monuments and wonders of the world were built by people who were organized in large teams by a domination system. Think what wonders might be built by a cooperation system. The foundations of a new and collaborative wonder are being drawn now, teams are multiplying exponentially, the celebration of new vision and camaraderie are reverberating like whale songs under the storm-driven waves, and everyone is welcome, including you.

The times they are a-changin'
(Bob Dylan, 1963)

There is a peaceful, new American Revolution in progress, a cultural recovery process, where more and more people are looking at their personal lifestyle choices and making new choices that reflect their own values rather than accepting those of the consumer mainstream. For example, in the 2004 election, of all eligible voters only 31 percent approved of Mr. Bush, only 28 percent approved of Mr. Kerry, and an overwhelming 44 percent approved of absolutely nobody by not voting in an election which was touted as crucial to the future of the nation. The major political parties have not recognized this nation-within-a-nation as a people whose needs for leadership have not been fulfilled. The politicians appear to be unable to adapt to a rapidly changing political environment, somewhat like slow-moving dinosaurs.

The dissatisfaction with traditional politics, and the desire for integrity and authenticity that is neither left nor right, is one of the profile characteristics of these new revolutionaries, described by Paul Ray and

---

[63] http://www.yesmagazine.org/article.asp?ID=1408

Sherry Anderson in their book *"The Cultural Creatives."* [64] Other characteristics include a deep caring for the planetary ecosystems, social justice, and peace, as well as intentions to create real intimacy in relationships with others, oneself and with a spiritual source. Ray describes cultural creatives as "deep green and out in front" when it comes to politics. They are less likely to just talk about change and more likely to volunteer to do something to make it happen.

They have redefined success to mean personal and social actualization instead of corporate materialism. They avoid cynicism and negativity, they have found hope. However, they are unaware that there are millions of other people just like themselves. In fact, Ray and Anderson estimated that in the year 2000 there were over 50 million cultural creatives in America and 90 million in Europe who had independently arrived at the same shift in values. Are we witnessing the 100th monkey syndrome? The booms in socially responsible investing, sustainable agriculture, and alternative health care are just some of the economic indicators of this shift in values.

Ray and Anderson's thesis is that "a creative minority can have enormous leverage to carry us into a new renaissance instead of a disastrous fall." Ray has surveyed the change in values that has taken place in America over the last 40 years, and talks about the potential of the New Progressives in *"The New Political Compass."* [65] One of his most hope-filled diagrams of this compass illustrates that an estimated 36% of the population and 45% of potential voters (not actual voters) are out in front on the crucial issues of survival, separate from the conventional division of left and right, and are definitely opposed to big business.

This rapidly changing set of values is further illustrated by the 40% of Americans in 2003 who rated dealing with the nation's energy problem or protection of the environment as a top priority. Their numbers grew to 58% of the population in 2006 (Pew Research Center). In 1995, 89% of Americans agreed that buying and consuming is the American way (Merck Family Fund), and only 9 years later, that percentage had dropped to 40% (Center for a New American Dream).

Negative news feeds our egotistical desire to feel superior. The positive news gets drowned out, so we have to look for it. My favorite source of hopeful news is YES! magazine, which in 2010 cited ten hopeful trends. Briefly restated, these trends are:

1. Climate crisis response is coming from the grassroots.
2. The veil of government secrecy is being broken.
3. Momentum is building for abolition of nuclear weapons.
4. Resilience is being built at the local level.
5. Health care for all is being considered.
6. Corporate power is being challenged.
7. A local economy movement is taking off.
8. Cooperatives are making a comeback.
9. Homophobia is being exposed.
10. Social movements are connecting the dots, building in size. [66]

---

[64] Ray, P. & Anderson, S., The Cultural Creatives: how 50 million people are changing the world, Harmony Books 2000. See also: http://www.culturalcreatives.org/faq.html

[65] http://www.grassrootsforamerica.us/fertilizer/New-Political-Compass-Intro.shtml

[66] http://www.yesmagazine.org/blogs/sarah-van-gelder/10-most-hopeful-stories-of-2010

Even earlier, in 2006, YES! magazine listed these increasing trends:

1. active nonviolence as a tool for peace and justice,
2. organic, local, sustainable agriculture,
3. efforts to protect Earth's ecosystems,
4. political art,
5. the idea that the Universe has a direction and purpose,
6. resistance to corporate advertising,
7. insistence on the rights of indigenous peoples,
8. awareness of the need to reclaim democracy,
9. progressives using the internet to work for justice issues,
10. humility, learning from other species and cultures. [67]

Change is coming rapidly, and if we look for positive changes we can find them. We have the world-wide internet, cell phones in wide use in isolated corners of the world, artists communicating transcendent feelings with video and music, and a huge grassroots defiance of the politics of fear and control that is expanding exponentially. "The other superpower," a phrase coined by the New York Times to describe the world peace movement and the February 2003 demonstrations, is a real and surprising authority for commanding, and indeed enforcing, a ceasefire.

Years of research and development have been devoted to the field of conflict resolution. The humiliating collapse of the Soviet Union and the precarious economic state of the United States and the European Union are forcing the increasing localization of energy and food production. Stronger communities are evolving.

There is a growing awareness that forcefully grabbing resources results in a net loss.

We are the system

Systems theory has become an interdisciplinary science in many fields, including geography, sociology, political science, organizational theory, management, psychotherapy (within family systems therapy), and economics. In grad school, I studied systematic design planning, and the primary lesson I still carry with me is that the complete and thorough description of a problem contains the description of its solution. Our discipline was to make endless analysis lists, not only of goals and barriers, but also of resources and alternatives. The synthesis, the solution, emerged from the analysis, and more often than not that emergence was intuitive, elegant, and simple. This is the essence of systems theory, to see the big picture -- the hidden structure and pattern -- rise up into view from the tiny details.

One of my heroes is R. Buckminster Fuller,[68] whom you may know as the designer of the geodesic dome. I heard him speak in 1968 at Ohio State University, and the students gave him a well-deserved standing ovation. Fuller was a maverick genius who was thinking holistically in the 1920's and 1930's. He saw the world as a global village, and took on the task of enumerating the ratio of energy and resources to people in tools like a World Energy Map, illustrating the growing differences between the rich and poor as a source for socialist revolution. Fuller once said,

"communication between all peoples anywhere...is approximately 186,000 miles per second. In terms

[67] http://www.yesmagazine.org/issues/10-most-hopeful-trends/table-of-contents

[68] http://www.bfi.org/

of mores, languages, politics, they are as yet months, years, and generations apart. In terms of human needs and longings of understanding, they are as one."

One of my other maverick genius heroes is the Bolivian mystic, Oscar Ichazo, who invented trialectics[69] to explain that change does not occur through dialectical conflict of opposites, but through attraction to higher levels of sophistication. Thus change is inevitable and evolutionary. Recovery from violence will not happen on a large scale just because it should, or because it is moral or just. It will occur because we are drawn to the joy, peace, and satisfaction of people living together in intimate harmony. The singing and dancing will relentlessly speak to our hearts. And our thoughts about it, our analysis, will drift away. So, the most productive way to cope with unacceptable conditions is to take responsibility for one's own participation in the system, to change oneself, to "be the change you want to see," as Gandhi said.

I see systems theory as overlapping with the mystical inspirations of the world's religions. Consider that they all assert in differing ways a fundamental unifying principle that *we are one,* that humanity moves forward as a single system, and that all separation is an illusion. Therefore, we cannot be opposed to the system if we *are* the system and wish to survive. So, if we are having a negative experience and we can see ourselves as inseparable from the system we find ourselves in, we have to ask ourselves, are we victims of the system or are we perceiving the system from our victim stance? I quote from Gene Bellinger's systems-thinking web site:

Experience has taught us well to react to events and to respond to patterns of behavior. Yet, there is a deeper level of understanding possible. An understanding on the level of structure. There are underlying structures responsible for the patterns of behavior and the events. Our lack of awareness of these structures often makes us the victim of them, even though many of the structures are of our own creation. The structures are not hidden, they are simply not obvious. We have never developed a way to see and understand them. Once we become aware of structures, how to look for them, and understand them, they become readily apparent all around us. [70]

When we see our place in the grand scheme of things, we are more likely to become active participants in solving what otherwise might seem to be overwhelming problems. The most subversive activity to the status quo is the use of imagination. There *are* new possibilities if we but look for them.

For example, when it comes to alternative strategies to create peace through strength or strength through peace, the list can become very long. For openers, how about promoting family harmony with domestic violence prevention programs? That's a form of strength and a form of peace. When we start teaching parents and children win-win solutions to conflict in the home, valuable lessons are generalized to other conflicts and an important piece is added to a culture of peace, stability, and security.

When we can teach our children, our parents, our teachers, our gang members, our

---

[69] http://www.tomislavbudak.com/trialectics.htm

[70] http://www.systems-thinking.org/vossov/vos.htm

prisoners, our police and military, our politicians and diplomats, and our corporate boards that having power *with* others is far more creative and effective than having power *over* others, we will begin to see the crisis of violence in our nation and our world subside.

We will see conflict resolution skills developed into a high art at all levels. The funds that are now being consumed in vast amounts to deal with interpersonal and systemic violence crises will be available for the healthy growth and development of children as well as the true security and prosperity of adults -- worldwide!

The genius that is needed to ensure our survival will not emerge until we give it the space to be. Genius does not emerge easily in a critical, competitive environment. Rapid adoption of the much-needed ideas coming from genius requires a new kind of respect from an entire society.

Optimists have more fun

I grew up terrified of my father's physical abuse, nuclear bombs, and the selective service board that denied my conscientious objection. I became an angry, alienated, and apathetic young man. I had a self-righteous belief in the ultimate selfishness and separateness of human beings. I was cynical to the extreme. I became locked into a self-destructive cycle, and in 1985 I was forced to ask as so many of us have, what am I living for? Today, I feel very much alive, and I have a deep need to contribute to the end of violence. On my return journey, my pilgrimage back to life, I am learning how to be connected to a spiritual source, a community of loving human beings, and myself. I am learning that I am part of a much greater whole and that I am the only one responsible for my attitude. I have accepted that no matter how small my efforts seem to be, they still have a cumulative effect on systemic change.

I once had an epiphany about my cynicism. I saw that it came from my desire to fix and control others' behavior and the obvious impossibility of doing so. I believe America's current political paradigm is based on the need for control and is thus unavoidably cynical. For example, some people wish for "peace" but take no personal responsibility for creating it, expecting the government to fix and control those "other people," all the while not believing that anybody will.

However, by not opposing or resisting anyone, by getting people involved in dialogue, immersed in thoughts of creating a solution, we can participate in a living laboratory of democratic learning. We can experiment with faith in others. We can practice courage with heartfelt convictions, and surrender to the overall process. This is what it takes for a small group to plant the roots of a culture of peace. And as the culture of peace grows it will become a reality for everyone.

Only when something truly stunning happens such as the shooting of Representative Giffords in Arizona do we dare to ask fundamental questions about our culture of violence. How is it that we get blindsided by such violence and never see it coming?

"Only a crisis – actual or perceived – produces real change. When that crisis occurs, the actions that are taken depend on the ideas that are lying around. That, I believe, is our basic function: to develop alternatives to existing policies, to keep them alive and available until the politically impossible becomes politically inevitable."
-- Milton Friedman

Perhaps in this crisis we will finally be motivated to begin the baby steps toward a culture of violence prevention, and some day before we commit national suicide authorize a

Department of Peace which would teach and implement advanced conflict resolution skills within the USA and complement military defense with greatly enhanced diplomacy and development overseas. Now, I mostly agree with those who say peace cannot come *from* government, and what is to stop us from giving peace *to* government?

We can start right here, right now. Find someone whom you believe to be your political enemy, and take them to lunch. Listen to each other, suspend judgment, ask about the hardships and struggles that have shaped beliefs, ask about what's really important and find the values you agree on. It will take some time, some practice, some real effort and genuine courage to do what we have never done before: disarm ourselves, create community and look without blinking at our own resistance to peace with our neighbor.

> *"It takes more courage to reveal insecurities than hide them, more strength to relate to people than to dominate them, more 'manhood' to abide by thought-out principles rather than blind reflex. Toughness is in the soul and spirit, not in muscles and an immature mind."* -- Alex Karras

Since I decided to play a role in the creation of world peace, I have been burning with a deliciously impatient obsession. I cannot sleep at night sometimes, I get so excited. Sometimes, I wrestle with my own doubts. Then there are those rare moments in meditation when I am swept into wordless feelings of loving support, and I shed tears of joy. At such times, it seems impossible for me to be discouraged.

I have to discipline myself to see problems as opportunities, which is so much better than feeling stuck in the misery and self-

pity of problems as barriers. This peace process is transforming me into a better person. My participation is about becoming part of the process, not about creating the result. The result is completely shrouded. I do not know the outcome. For me, the truly important things do not occur in space and time, they occur in our hearts.

My heart's desire is to give you hope, for hope is a powerful source -- perhaps *the* single most powerful source -- of energy for change. Acting as if a goal is inevitable unleashes hope and creative energy, and I am speaking from my personal experience. For example, if you look for them, there are thousands of electric vehicle enthusiasts, some with degrees in engineering or physics, some with high school diplomas, toiling away in their warehouses and garages, experimenting with the new frontier of electric transportation. That daring provides encouragement for others like myself. Observing their efforts moved me from daydreams to certainty. I decided to risk building my own electric vehicle, below. I've put over 4,500 miles on it in 3 years, just running errands around town. [71]

> *"It is not because things are difficult that we do not dare; it is because we do not dare that they are difficult."* -- Seneca, Roman philosopher

---

[71] http://www.xp-humm-e.info

I believe another world, a world where conflict is resolved without violence, is not only possible, it is being created right now, and it is time to join the parade.

What do you think? Do you think wars are inevitable? What are your hopes? What kind of world do you want to live in? Perhaps the most important question is: What are you willing to do about it?

In 1976 I wrote my first book, instructions on how to build a wood-strip canoe. In the introduction, I wrote some words of encouragement directed toward a first-time boatbuilder, and today I find these same words still apply to my life as I move forward in learning what it is I can do. I don't know yet. I am re-learning that being "out of control" is a blessed state in which I am willing to receive what the Universe is giving me. I don't have to have the whole step-by-step directions to a guaranteed destination. Building canoes and building peace have a common need for a surrender to the process.

"The first thing I want to tell you is DO IT. This book is not the experience; you have to create that. It is not the whole truth; it is only a map containing symbols for the reality which is in the process and in you. Allow the boat to come out of you the way it wants to come out, not the way you think it is supposed to come out. The way things are supposed to be is not the way things ARE. The fantasy I have in my mind of the boat I might build does not, will not, look like the boat I will actually build. I guarantee you that. It will be pointed at both ends and it will float, all right, but all the events and contingencies that occur during the process of building are going to keep changing what the boat finally looks like. The finished boat is in you, in your body. You can't see it, visualize it, imagine, until it happens. OK? You cannot imagine the grain structure of the interior of a board or a tree; you can only see it after it has been cut open." [72]

The design for peace is ready, let's build it. We can change history so that peace is no longer impossible, it becomes inevitable!

The really important things don't happen in space and time, they happen in our hearts. Think with your heart, Peace is waiting for you there. Give yourself to Peace, and you become the Gift. Your Gift is the breath that blows the seed of passionate Love to Earth.

I invite you to a brief ceremony of gratitude.

Imagine for a moment that only a few miles above you there is no atmosphere, only empty space and stars.

Imagine for a moment the earth beneath your feet as your Mother, source of all your nourishment.

Feel for a moment the blessing that is your life.

Feel for a long moment your ability to bring blessing to this planet.

In gratitude, we say Amen for all that is.

---

[72] Hazen, D., The Stripper's Guide to Canoe-building, Tamal Vista, 6th edition, 1999.

Cliff notes for self-activation

Nobody plans their recovery -- or do they?

> We rarely reach the point of arranging for our own self-change.
>
> > *"The developing personality obeys only brute necessity."* -- C. Jung
>
> People are best motivated by pain, when their life is shit.
>
> Nobody admits they *chose* to drop out of school, wreck their cars, go to jail, divorce, lose their children, their health, jobs, and friends -- but that's what they actually did!
>
> Nobody claims that *surviving* crisis has something to do with their innate strengths and value to others -- but it does!

We have a buried wisdom inside of us, an internal life-force.

> **You did not create yourself or will your addiction.**
>
> > We do not belong to ourselves, we found ourselves here as the expression of a life-force that we don't know.
> >
> > Our bodies are awesomely complicated and beautiful.
> >
> > We do not will our hearts to beat, our lungs to breathe.
> >
> > We cannot will ourselves to be other than what we are.
>
> **You only have stewardship of your body.**
>
> > All we really own is our time, thoughts, and behavior, or in other words, our process, our internal selves.
> >
> > All of what we think we own or our context -- our external selves -- are transitory, vain, and false.

> The physical self is the tool for the education of the meta-physical self (mind, emotions, "spirit") contained within it.

We have forgotten our true nature.

> We live in a culture that is materialistic, externally-referenced, paternalistic (authoritarian) and discouraging to "irrational" spiritual growth.
>
> Human *beings* have become human *doings* because of low self-esteem and the focus on not making "mistakes."
>
> > Our high technology produces garbage because we put garbage into it. We can go to the moon, but we can't communicate!
>
> Our minds have become hyper-vigilant, tyrannical defenders of our bodies, which are only the temporary carriages for our spirits. Our minds are *not* our masters. Our deepest values, our spirit, our consciousness, is the true master.
>
> Sales people know that all real decisions are emotional and irrational.
>
> Addiction can be seen as an attempt to escape the rational mind, a craving for spiritual awareness.
>
> > It's easier in the short term to be a cowboy (illusion of control) than to make the effort to be a rose with long-term survival (acceptance).
>
> Acceptance (honesty) is more powerful at removing fear, guilt and worry than any possible means of control.

Our intellect is both our Best Friend and Biggest Obstacle to Growth.

> The mind is a powerful tool for organizing information into patterns by noticing similarities and differences, details.

New perceptions are always fitted into old perceptions.

Paradigm shifts, whole-pattern "override programs," are difficult to install, requiring us to hold down the "on" button for new programming of our perception.

Unfortunately, as information becomes more complex, it is easier to notice differences, missing components, and negative features.

You only see Yourself, the Exterior is You.

Our perceptions are filtered and colored by our entire life history of learning. Everything is subjective.

Everywhere you go, there your negativity is.

> *We have met the enemy, and he is us.*
> -- Pogo, by Walt Kelly

We are trapped by our own self-limiting beliefs and attitudes, not by someone or something outside of ourselves.

New evidence suggests that our attitudes exist at the cellular level and predispose us to heart attacks, cancer, illness of all kinds.

What we resist, persists, causing depression and exhaustion.

When we try to control what we cannot control, we lose control over the things that we can control (thoughts and behavior).

Depression is a loss of control of thoughts and a direct cause of physical headaches.

Depression is an attempt to control, a refusal to face a crisis and die a mini-death, putting the crisis on hold with analysis-paralysis and self-pity.

Depression is anger turned inward.

Minimal mental activity combined with high emotional involvement and physical activity produces serenity and joy.

Life is a Test on Learning How to Love.

Near-death research indicates that a pop quiz probably occurs moments after you are clinically dead. (What did you learn about and do with love?)

Awareness of our mortality empowers us to live true to our deepest values and to experience our vitality more fully.

Spirituality and recovery begins with the internal freedom that comes with believing that we are capable and lovable.

Recovery is also coming home to the natural self, and having the answers to three vital questions: Who am I? Who am I with? Where am I going?

A Crisis is an Opportunity to Learn, to Wake Up.

Chinese word for "crisis" is combination of two characters, "danger" and "opportunity."

Crisis is a threat of loss or an actual loss which arouses anxiety, grief, guilt, anger, depression, or craziness.

The felt danger is the loss of our dreams and false pride.

The pain of the crisis evokes a strong desire to run to the old and familiar behaviors, no matter how dysfunctional.

> The real danger is the loss of our true self if we believe we are isolated, unteachable, that our life is a "mistake."

The grief, guilt, and anger provide the fuel, the energy, to break out of the cocoon and learn to fly.

Our problems are our stepping stones to freedom.

Anyone who does the work for the caterpillar (enables) robs it of the strength it would have gained from the struggle.

See the Grief for your Cocoon.

Usually people feel worse before feeling better.

The caterpillar has no idea that it is going to be a butterfly.

The loss at first appears meaningless, to be endured, ignored, anesthetized, or avoided.

What was once our security or even our delight is now a chain around our neck.

Learning is the painful reorganization of what we thought we knew.

We are being forced to discover inner resources that we are not aware of and do not know how to use.

Our old "friends" and our family cannot understand what we are facing. We feel isolated, and we are.

Of course we are angry!

Roses grow best in shit!

Growing up is Learning How to Learn.

Maturation is the process of becoming involved with ourselves and the changes we go through, so that we see "the big picture."

As we grow, we move from dependence to independence, from needy to giving, from negative to positive, from rigid to flexible, from unrealistic to realistic, from clever to simple, from fear to wisdom, from suffering to harmony.

Ability to Learn is based on Self-Esteem

Self-esteem gives us the durability to roll with the punches.

Awareness of strengths *and* limitations is true self-respect, allowing us to accept ourselves as human, teachable.

I am lovable, worthwhile, useful, purposeful.

I am significant, I belong, my impact spreads beyond others.

"Life..(is)..a very great gift...not because of what it gives us, but because of what it enables us to give others." -- Thomas Merton

I am capable, I will survive, I *have* survived, I have learned.

Self-Esteem is Humility and Love.

Humility is a sense of belonging to a larger system than ourselves, having a Higher Power, acknowledging our limits.

LOVE = Letting Old Vanity Evaporate.

Ego games of fear and control are opposed to love.

I am fallible, I don't know everything, I'm not perfect.

I am learning how to love myself and others.

I am grateful for this opportunity to learn.

Check your expectations, your "old" mind-set.

Self-honesty produces insight and harmony with new reality.

Frustrated expectations are the only cause of stress

Can I change my expectations to be more flexible?

Learn to love each other, and you will get the love you need.

No effort of the self can remove the self from its own self-centeredness.

-- William Temple

If you are lonely, your best friend is another lonely person.

Accepting others as mirrors for ourselves (compassion) allows us to believe that we

have been accepted, supported, and
guided, so that we can take risks (action).

Practice listening.

Listening produces a safe space for others.

Trust others' process - they can/will learn
and change.

Feedback should be specific, helpful, brief,
objective.

Avoid giving advice!

You have everything you need

...and it is indestructible.
Consciousness, spirit lives forever.

Trust the Process, there is NO RETREAT

Humanity evolves as a unitary body,
relentlessly moving.

Lessons will be repeated until learned.
The only real mistake is to give up.

When we make mistakes, it shows that
we are willing to try.

There are no problems, only undefined
situations. We must learn to live with
partial knowledge, partial power,
partial freedom.[73]

You can run, but you can't hide.
Suicide is not an option.

*Increased intuition -- letting go of
rational control -- is both the process
and the goal.*

The Crisis is a signal from our internal self

The God or life-force within us is ready to
grow.

---

[73] Kopp, S.B., PhD., If you meet the Buddha on the road, kill him! Lowe & Brydon (Printers) Ltd. 1974.